D0529483

Think Smart—Act Smart

Think Smart—
Act Smart

Avoiding the Business
Mistakes That Even
Intelligent People Make

JIM NIGHTINGALE

BICENTENNIAL
1807
WILEY
2007
BICENTENNIAL

John Wiley & Sons, Inc.

Copyright © 2008 by John Wiley & Sons, Inc. All rights reserved.

Published by John Wiley & Sons, Inc., Hoboken, New Jersey.

Published simultaneously in Canada.

Wiley Bicentennial Logo: Richard J. Pacifico.

For general information on our other products and services, or technical support, please contact our Customer Care Department within the United States at 800–762–2974, outside the United States at 317-572-3993 or fax 317-572-4002.

Wiley also publishes its books in a variety of electronic formats. Some content that appears in print may not be available in electronic books.

For more information about Wiley products, visit our Web site at http://www.wiley.com.

Library of Congress Cataloging-in-Publication Data:

Nightingale, Jim, 1960–
    Think smart—act smart: avoiding the business mistakes that even intelligent people make / Jim Nightingale.
        p. cm.
    Includes bibliographical references and index.
    ISBN 978-0-470-17129-5 (cloth)
1. Decision making.   2. Errors.   3. Management.   I. Title.
HD30.23.N525 2008
658.4′03—dc22   2007022148

Printed in the United States of America

10 9 8 7 6 5 4 3 2 1

To my wife

Contents

Preface

I f this book had a hero, it would probably be Sir Isaac Newton. Today there is an entire branch of physics known as Newtonian. Newton made great discoveries in mathematics, optics, and physics, and his formulation of the law of gravitation is still in use today. By the age of 23, he had developed a workable version of calculus, and his thinking was ahead of any other mathematician in Europe. As president of the Royal Society, Newton became the world's first great administrator of science, laying the foundation for the way research is conducted today.

In short, Newton was a true genius. Not just a very smart guy, but the real deal, a man who could, by sheer force of intellect, uncover the deepest mysteries of nature.

Yet, as this book will describe, when Newton deduced that a crash in England's young stock market was inevitable, he chose not to withdraw from the market and lost the equivalent of over a million dollars (in today's money). He later commented "I can predict the motions of the planets, but not the limits of human folly. " His mistake looked much like that made by many investors in America's dot.com crash.

Sometimes apparently intelligent individuals, even geniuses, do things that look exactly like stupidity. That is what this book is about.

In general, we don't worry about smart people making stupid decisions. We believe that having smart people involved in an enterprise means things will turn out well. Smart people are well paid. Corporations, the government, and academia seek them out for their talent. When things go wrong, we look for smart people to fix them. Why? Because we think that they will get it right.

Yet if we look around us, we can find all kinds of examples of things that smart people got wrong. In hindsight, some of them seem so simple. We look at them and say, "How could a smart guy like him do something so stupid?" The Ford Edsel was created by some of Detroit's best automobile brains, men who achieved great success both before and after that debacle. Similarly, the Bay of Pigs invasion was approved and executed by a group of individuals who were supposedly America's "best and brightest," yet it was laughably ill conceived and poorly thought through. How did the space shuttle *Challenger* crash when, looking back, the data and causes were so obvious? How many of us have asked ourselves why such a wonderful person as our friend is dating such a loser when the entire rest of the planet knows she deserves better?

The list of high-profile stupidities committed by intelligent individuals is endless. The examples come from all aspects of society. The commercial arena, for instance, gives us examples like the never-ending stream of management fads it has embraced since the 1980s, the buying behavior of the investing public during the dot.com runup of the 1990s, and the Long-Term Capital Management disaster where Nobel Prize winners collaborated in the destruction of a successful hedge fund. Every segment of society has offered up gems of idiocy, or at least something that looks like idiocy, for our consideration.

This book is about why these things happen, and why they have to happen, at least until we understand their causes. All the errors presented in this book were caused by ways of thinking that are not stupid; indeed, we need them in order to live. But like many good things, too much of them can be harmful.

There are trade-offs in ways of thinking, just like in anything else. If I buy a car that is big and comfortable, I have to spend more on gas; if I buy a small, fuel-efficient car, I lose in safety.

The same trade-offs apply to the ways we think. For example, if we are wired to value associations with other people, if we are to be pack creatures and have to obtain crucial support from our fellows, we will sometimes make mistakes by "going along with the crowd" because we value our group membership so highly. Every error in this book is the result of this kind of trade-off; they are good things gone bad. Each one is an example of a behavior we need but that sometimes leads us to error.

The study of error is probably as old as the human race. It has been said that humanity advances every time a person comes to understand something he hadn't before and with each "Eureka!" we get a little smarter. But it also progresses with every "Well, that stung. Not going to try that again!"

Certainly if we couldn't learn from our mistakes, humanity's time on this planet would have been very short, but there is a larger unknown about errors, which is: Why do we make them in the first place? And there's the even more frustrating question: Why do smart people sometimes do such stupid things?

When I was fresh out of school, educated as a nuclear engineer, I went to work for a local utility in Chicago. It was a big company, and a leader, at least in terms of size, in building and operating nuclear power plants with all the complex technology that involves. After a brief stint as a trainer, I went to work helping to build and test a new plant. I was surrounded by smart people, everyone involved was intelligent, educated, and many were already experienced in the power industry. Yet all was not well.

Time and again I saw us make mistakes that we should have avoided, not "China Syndrome" material, but things that kept us from bringing the plant on line as planned. I could never figure out how we could be so smart and so stupid at the same time. Later, when I entered the consulting field, I found that some other companies running similar nuclear programs were able to do much better, and some were much worse. Yet they all had smart people. When my consulting work took me outside the power industry, I saw that same thing in other areas.

In some ways being part of the nuclear power industry was very educational. One facet of my involvement in that industry was being a bit on the inside of the public debate that went on over the safety of the technology. There were clearly smart people on both sides of the debate, yet some thought that this technology was literally the end of the world, and others felt it was its salvation. If they couldn't both be right, how could they both be smart? As an engineer working on the plants, I was nominally on the pro side, but I tried to understand everyone's arguments.

One particular incident stuck with me. In the latter stages of plant construction, there was a finding of low-level radioactivity in the local water supply. The uproar was immediate. The anti-nuclear activists were furious; the plant was not even running yet and already it was polluting the local environment. There were protests and articles in the local papers. Those inside the plant were equally incensed. At that time there was not a gram of nuclear fuel on the site. The reason for the low level of radioactivity in the local water was that the plant was being built over an abandoned coal mine, and coal has a certain natural radioactivity, which had always been in the water on that site and always would be. We perceived the protesters as cynical. How could they not know what they were doing? It was so simple, they were obviously telling a bold-faced lie to drum up press coverage. At the time, I could not conceive that they could actually believe what they were saying.

I now believe that the anti-nuclear crowd, at least most members, were probably sincere, just mistaken in this case. They were neither stupid nor dishonest, but the victims of some of the thought patterns you will discover in this book.

This type of incident interested me enough to look into the psychology of belief and the process of how humans make decisions. What I found startled me. The errors that I had noticed in the business world paled next to some of the weird things that people believe in everyday life. How on earth can people convince themselves, as members of the Heaven's Gate group did, that if they committed suicide, an alien spaceship would transport them to heaven? Most of us just shrug; those people were just weird, after all. Yet the Heaven's Gate people held jobs, raised children, and generally functioned in society; they were not idiots. The more I thought about it, the more all these mistakes started to look alike to me. Even some of the beliefs in left field were rooted in the same type of thought processes that made the smartest engineers and managers I knew do things wrong.

As my career progressed and I began working with more senior people, I noticed that the business world did not really have a handle on why people make mistakes in judgment and provided very little training in how to avoid them.

As I continued to look at this problem, a few things became clear to me. These are the points I will discuss in this book.

- The thought patterns that make smart people do stupid things are rooted in our own evolution and development. These thought patterns are not evil or stupid—they are just inappropriate.
- The mistakes that important scientists, government leaders, and business managers make, those that look like subtle misjudgments, are driven by the same thought patterns as those made by the most ridiculously stupid of our fellows, those who win Darwin Awards.

- Intelligence does not prevent these mistakes, at least not perfectly. Indeed, being smart actually seems to make you more susceptible to certain types of error.

I have divided these mistakes into four major groups according to the underlying psychological forces behind them:

1. **Wishful thinking.** Strong desire makes it difficult for us to think clearly and realistically.
2. **Mythical thinking.** We are unable to free ourselves from powerfully held beliefs that explain the world for us and to which we have made strong commitments, or are unable to discard an approach that has been successful for us in the past.
3. **Tribal thinking.** Social concerns keep us from reaching correct conclusions.
4. **Royal thinking.** Issues of power and hierarchy keep us from making good decisions.

The first two groups contain things that happen to individuals; the last two apply mostly to group situations, where several people are involved in the thinking process.

Some of these problems are more common in certain environments than others. For instance, mythical thinking is about being unable to change a belief or way of looking at the world. In the commercial world, there are immediate economic consequences for mistakes, and these consequences keep us from indulging in mythical thinking as much as we can in, say, a government or military bureaucracy. In a for-profit organization, a mistake might survive for months or sometimes years before being corrected, but in general, it does not take too long before the board of directors starts talking about a "change of direction," meaning a change in leadership, and things get fixed. In the bureaucratic world of government, the same kind of mistaken beliefs can hang on for decades.

This book is supposed to be for everybody, and to be useful it has to focus mainly on case studies of the behaviors in question. I have drawn these from a number of sources, including military, academic, and government organizations, but the largest number come from the business world, the world that I think would derive the greatest benefit from a book like this. Besides the case studies, the text also includes some explanation and analysis.

Finally I need to acknowledge that it takes a certain arrogance to write about other people's mistakes, especially when those people are all smarter than you are. In the spirit of full disclosure, I claim no immunity from these mistakes myself and have fallen prey to each of them at one time or another (many times actually). My aim in this book is to point out some interesting things that I think have not been said in this way before and perhaps make it a fun read, but I claim no "guru-hood" and freely admit to being as smart and as dumb as the next guy.

Acknowledgements

I have always wondered about the long list of people authors thank in their acknowledgements. Surely so many people couldn't have made real contributions to the essentially solitary task of writing, I thought. This, of course, was before I began adding up the people to whom I am indebted for the creation of this work. There is my wife, Cathy Busking, who was my chief consultant, thinking partner, meal ticket, and everything else. There are also my parents, Sam and Barbara Nightingale, from whom I learned both the English language and the trick of stubborn endurance until a task is completed that is essential to writing a book.

There are also a number of wonderful people who took time from their own pursuits to give me counsel on this book. Thanks to Mary Jean Busking, Lucia Nacimento, Marta Cappa, Jack Dawson, Matt Thompson, and Beth Bartolinni.

Lastly, thanks to everyone who had the courage to go out and try something they didn't know exactly how to accomplish, thus risking failure. Every error in this book happened because somebody had the care and courage to take a chance. Thus we progress.

CHAPTER 1

Avoiding Error: An Introduction

This chapter is written for professional decision makers, who generally work in some kind of organization. They are managers and leaders and what they do for a living is decide things. If you're reading this book for your own benefit, you might want to skip to the "habits" section later in this chapter, where there are some suggestions for personal decision making. If you just want to read the stories about smart guys doing stupid things, go ahead and skip to Chapter 2.

There are no easy countermeasures for the errors described in this book. They are complex mistakes with their roots deep in the way our minds are constructed. But we can learn to avoid them.

To begin with, there are three basic characteristics of decision making that need to be understood:

1. **Most decisions are made unconsciously.** That is, we don't think "Here is a decision for me to make, I will now make the decision." Instead, we simply decide without thinking much about the decision process. When the question of who should work on a new project comes up, we unconsciously weigh the options and suggest a candidate. Unless it is unusually important, we don't explicitly sit down to "make a decision."

   This point is important, because much of the coaching that managers receive about decision making is focused on techniques. For instance, the instructor or consultant will provide a way to weigh the pros and cons of alternatives against each other to determine which approach is correct. This is perfectly fine, and there are places for this kind of technique, especially in formal decision-making processes. But frankly, if you tried to use them regularly, you would be fired in a month because they take too much time.

2. **The techniques don't address the major problem facing many organizations: getting decision makers to see the world through the right lens**—that is, to give the appropriate weight to the right things. If the challenge facing the organization is quality, then getting people to see the world through the lens of quality is the true work of leadership. This point is discussed later in this chapter in the section on goals.

3. **There isn't a single right way to make decisions.** In the preface, I presented the four areas where smart people make spectacularly bad decisions, mentioning that most of the time, the kind of thinking that drives these errors isn't harmful, and actually serves us pretty well. Consider the positive side to each type of error.

    1. **Wishful thinking.** In this type of thinking, strong desire makes it difficult for us to think well. The dot.com stock run-up is the typical error here. Hordes of smart people bet on unproven new technologies because the upside seemed so large. Wishful thinking is clearly something we need to eliminate, isn't it? Well, just a moment. Wishful thinking is just the dark side of optimism, the general belief that we can make things turn out well. Psychologists who study optimism tell us that the people at the top of almost every field are optimists. This is because each time they fail, they try again, secure in the belief that eventually they'll get it right.

       Optimism is a fundamental survival trait for human beings. Without it we never would have made it out of the caves. Only an optimist would look at a buffalo and say "I'm gonna kill that thing and eat it." The fact that the first few individuals who tried probably ended up trampled into the landscape does not diminish the value of optimism as a trait.

       Sometimes an organization loses its optimism. This happens when it fails repeatedly, when people are laid off, and when management does not seem to have the answers. If you have worked in this kind of organization, I pity you, because I have.

They are joyless places, without energy or aspirations, where people go through their daily tasks with a numb, rote fatalism that sucks the life out of anyone it touches.

2. **Mythical thinking.** Here we are unable to free ourselves from powerfully held beliefs that explain the world for us or strategies that have been successful in the past. We have all seen people hold fast to ideas after the time for change has come and gone. For instance, U.S. automakers had a terrible time understanding that consumers might not want big, gadget-laden cars and instead would prefer smaller, more efficient and reliable machines.

   The other side of the coin here is that we need these "worldviews" to make sense of the universe. People who make cars for a living have to have beliefs about what constitutes a good car, and sometimes they have to hold to these beliefs in the face of adversity.

   Banishing these structures altogether leaves an organization with no unifying culture or goals. Companies with weak worldviews or cultures tend to be opportunists, jumping on whatever looks profitable at the time. They are never thought leaders, and their lack of commitment prevents them from developing real core competencies.

3. **Tribal thinking.** Here social concerns keep us from reaching the correct conclusions. A great example of this error is the way companies chase after the latest management fad, simply because others are doing it. From quality circles to TQM (total quality management), the list is long and depressing. The problem isn't that these approaches don't have anything to offer; it's that managers pursue them as magic bullets instead of deeply understanding the business basics behind their (reputed) success and implementing them with care. This sheeplike, crowd-following behavior is not a substitute for leadership.

   Yet social groups are part of what makes us human. We are tribal animals, not loners, and organizations that don't value their own tribe don't work well internally and don't build coalitions with others. Almost anything worthy of time and effort today is too complex for a single person; we need our teams and tribes to accomplish our goals.

4. **Royal thinking.** Here issues of power and hierarchy keep us from making good decisions. A recent example of the way power and hierarchy can damage decision making can be seen in the way Saddam Hussein lost control of his own decision-making apparatus before and during the second Gulf War. Basically, anyone who brought Hussein bad news was killed, and thus he rarely heard the truth.

But organizations need some degree of hierarchy; someone has to make decisions. Organizations need leadership; someone has to be able to say "This is the way it is" so that people can go on with their duties, trusting that a person they respect is looking at the bigger picture. Someone needs to set goals and take responsibility in the face of uncertainty. Basically, the buck has to stop somewhere. The Hussein case is an example of power run amok, but that doesn't mean power is a bad thing.

Any organization needs a certain amount of confidence, a worldview of some strength, people who value being part of it, and a degree of hierarchy to function. But it can have too much of any of these characteristics. Exhibit 1.1 illustrates these traits along a spectrum, with the left side representing too much and the right side NOT ENOUGH. The mistakes described in this book are only at one end of the spectrum. In the exhibit, they occur on the

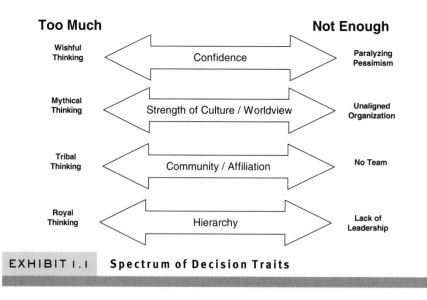

EXHIBIT I.I   **Spectrum of Decision Traits**

left-hand side, where the most spectacular errors happen. But an organization can be too far to the right-hand side also. In every case, for example, the question isn't How can I eliminate wishful thinking? Instead, the question is: Where do I want my organization to be on the continuum, and what processes need to be in place to help it succeed?

Think for a moment about an organization that continually turns out new products. Five years from now most of its revenue will be derived from products that are currently in a development pipeline (at best) or not yet conceived (at worst).

This organization needs a very confident decision style. It needs to be optimistic and comfortable taking risks. Thus it will score high in confidence and perhaps be prone to wishful thinking. Typically organizations like this have very limited hierarchies. Researchers and engineers are given a great deal of latitude and are managed by general goals instead of strict rules. You can't tell someone "You need to come up with three groundbreaking ideas this quarter." The company probably has a strong culture around innovation, and has the systems and processes in place to support it. While it may have a teamwork ethos, it will be tempered by healthy respect for individual initiative.

Contrast this with a company that creates its competitive advantage by being a least-cost producer. This company will score low in the confidence dimension, since it manages financial risk extremely closely and will probably have a strong culture and perhaps a strong hierarchy to enforce financial discipline.

Both these decision models are correct for the companies that have them, and each would be disastrous for the other.

Getting an organization to make the right decisions means working on a variety of processes, information systems, and human issues. Getting organizations to do this is not easy; in fact, it may be the most difficult thing most leaders ever have to do. To do this, we need to be disciplined and thoughtful in our thinking and to pay attention to a set of "rights" in decision making.

THE RIGHT GOALS

Among the most common decision pathologies in organizations are unclear goals. I once worked with the executive team of an entertainment company that provided a good illustration of this problem. Among the issues at hand were a series of bad decisions the team had made about customer service and a general tendency of the managers to bring everything to the top levels of the organization for approval, rather than taking the ball and running with it. Basically the team was not giving customer service the priority the chief executive officer (CEO) wanted it to have and was not being aggressive in making decisions.

For their part, members of the executive team claimed that whenever they made decisions on their own they were countermanded from above by the CEO and his inner circle. They didn't see how they could drive customer service, or anything else, until they were allowed to actually make decisions for themselves.

When I discussed this with the CEO, the problem became clear. The company had been near bankruptcy when he took the job, and he had centralized a lot of authority around spending to get control of costs. By this time, however, the situation had changed; the company was in decent shape financially and was ready to grow. Unfortunately, that message from the CEO had not been truly understood by his rather young management team, some of whom had not been part of a true leadership group in any environment other than one where the goal was struggling to survive. The managers were not making "bad" decisions; they just didn't understand what a "good" decision was.

Executives generally have two problems with communication. First, it's easy not to communicate enough. When you live with a problem every day, sometimes you assume that others are just as focused on it as you are. In reality, everyone has their own day-to-day issues to worry about, and if a goal, especially a new one, is not communicated clearly and regularly, people will forget about it.

Second, every organization has systems and procedures that tell employees what is important. These are things like where money is spent, who gets rewarded, who gets promoted, and what makes it to everyone's annual goals. Even if leaders communicate well, if they do not make sure the goal is clearly stated, the organization will decide that they don't really mean what they're saying and will continue to make bad decisions.

THE RIGHT INFORMATION (TO THE RIGHT PEOPLE AT THE RIGHT TIME)

It amazes me how much time managers (myself included) spend looking for information. We have a multitude of reports and binders full of data, yet we can never seem to find just the right view of the information at hand, so we manage by "intuition" or "feel." In the United States, managers generally would rather act than analyze, and we're terrified of paralysis by analysis. But at the same time we know the answer is out there and would rather find it than make it up if at all possible.

It is a lot harder for smart people to do something stupid if the right answer is there staring them in the face (although it's still very possible).

This is an area where technology can help. Techniques for automatically finding and presenting information from various sources have advanced to the point where today there is no reason why decision makers should not have access to all information that's available and pertinent to their needs. Unfortunately, many companies have not yet taken advantage of these technological advances, and doing so correctly is tougher than it looks.

Installing a system to provide key data to decision makers is not an information technology project. It looks like one from the outside, but it isn't. To do this correctly, you have to analyze the needs of every decision maker, the needs that are both well known and those that might emerge in the future. This means taking into account the organization's business strategy and looking beyond the decision to its implementation. In addition, you have to take into account the difference between raw data and useful information.

THE RIGHT PEOPLE

Often a bad decision comes about because the wrong people made it. They might be perfectly capable in some other area. In other words, they are not inept, just inapt. Or they might be the wrong group, incapable of working together effectively or bringing all the necessary skills and background to the table to get a good decision. In general, the right group for any decision will be one with three characteristics:

1. **It isn't too homogeneous.** Diversity is good in decision making, with some qualifiers. We aren't talking about ethnic diversity here, although sometimes there's a case for that; we're talking about diversity of experience. You need people with a broad range of experience to solve a difficult problem. If you don't have diversity, you don't have a group making a decision, you have the same person making it over and over.

2. **It isn't too timid.** Some of the worst decisions are made when one person or a small group dominates a decision-making group. People have to be able to speak up without fear of repercussions in order to be able to bring their experience to bear on the problem.

3. **It has the right skills.** Far too many decisions today are made by people removed from the effort, or who think they understand the issue but don't. Every decision-making group should include at least one person who lives with the question every day and knows all its ins and outs. This point may seem elementary, but it's often missed.

The Right Process

It may sound strange to talk about setting up processes for decision making; after all, we make decisions all the time without formal processes. Of course, we also we built things long before people figured out that systematizing the process with assembly lines and interchangeable parts made sense.

If you are going to have to make a particular type of decision over and over again, the best thing you can do is to formalize it.

Surprisingly, if you have an expert lay out a process for making a particular type of decision and then compare the expert's performance against that of a novice who is following the expert's process, often the novice outperforms the expert. What this means is that if a physician tells me and shows me exactly what to look for to diagnose a particular disease, and I follow those rules exactly, I might very well outperform the physician. In short, people are pretty good at creating decision rules but are pretty poor at following them.

In general, designing an effective decision-making process means making sure that the right people are involved and that certain steps are followed, and that constraints are set on what the decision can be (such as how much can be spent, who has to approve the decision, etc.).

The Right Habits

Making good decisions about complex issues, sometimes without enough information available, is not an art, nor is it a science. It is a discipline. Shortcuts are what often get people in trouble: making assumptions, failing to look at the other side, not doing the analysis that is available. After studying dozens of cases of very smart people making bad decisions, a few good practices became apparent. All the smart individuals featured in this book could have benefited from six rules:

1. **Look for disconfirming evidence.** Probably the single most important thing decision makers can do is look for evidence that tells them they're wrong. Of course, you can't do this until you have an idea of what your decision will be, but once you have a feel for that, you should look hard for things that can go wrong. Not only will this help you avoid bad decisions, but the thought process will help you in planning for contingencies.

   Some organizations look for disconfirming evidence through a risk analysis of important decisions, but this generally is kind of an afterthought, and most organizations don't do much with the analysis once it's completed. That's why it's important to include individuals on your team who are good at finding problems. They may slow down the process and keep you from getting to the decision you want quickly, but they will also help you get to a better one in the end.

2. **Do your homework.** Amazing as it may sound, many people don't do the simple data collection and analysis that could make a decision easy for them. They choose to rely on "feel" or the opinions of experts. Doing this may be good, but sometimes it's just relying on someone else's "feel." The discipline of building a business case has come into disrepute in business; this is because most managers can arrange for the outcome to be whatever they want it to be. But the fact that making a business case can be done badly doesn't change the fact that a good one is a key tool in making any effort successful.

3. **Stepping outside of the problem.** In the mid–1980s, Intel, which had pioneered the business of building computer memory chips, was slowly coming to the realization that these chips had become a commodity and that it could not compete with Japanese manufacturers on price. As profits dropped from $198 million in 1984 to less than $2 million in 1985, Andrew Grove, then president of Intel, recounts a conversation he had with CEO Gordon Moore regarding the problem:

   "I looked out the window at the Ferris wheel of the Great America amusement park revolving in the distance then I turned back to Gordon, and I asked 'If we got kicked out and the board brought in a new CEO, what do you think he would do?' Gordon answered without hesitation, 'He would get us out of memories.' I stared at him, numb, then said, 'Why shouldn't you and I walk out the door, come back, and do it ourselves?'"[1]

It can be very difficult to step outside a problem; maybe you were the one who made the decisions that got you in trouble in the first place, and admitting they were wrong reflects on your earlier judgment. But as the complexity of the decisions we make continues to increase with technology, there will be less and less room for allowing the past to intrude on the present. The ability to step away is a key decision skill for managers of complex undertakings.

4. **Review your decisions and see what worked and did not.** Very few people do this type of review as a matter of course. Most companies have processes for after-action reviews or lessons learned, but they are used only in exceptional circumstances, such as after a major project or after an epic failure.

   It is a lot of work to stop at the end of every week and ask yourself what you did right and wrong, and why, but some people manage to find the time, and the effort repays them, often profitably.

5. **Create a strong group of thinking partners.** It has been said that no man is an island, and nowhere is that more true than in making complex decisions. Of course, somebody has to make the final call, but up to that point almost everyone can benefit from good counsel. Most of the difficult problems that confront us today are too complex for a single individual to truly understand all the nuances. We need others to help us think and to provide alternative points of view.

   You probably know some people who are good thinking partners: They grasp the problem quickly, they listen, they question, and they challenge. You probably also know others who are not as good. These people may already have a solution in mind, or they may be uninterested in finding the truth, focusing rather on what the consequences of the decision will be for them.

   Most successful executives have key people they call on when making a big decision, and most of them spent a lot of time and effort building this group.

6. **Know your limits and beware of success.** Many high-profile errors come down to issues of confidence. Successful people are used to being right, and sometimes this can lead them to assume that they have grasped and understood a problem more quickly than they in fact have. Closely related to this is the fact that a lot of the cases in this book are rooted in previous success. When you are successful doing things a certain way, it can be hard to see how the world has changed and your old skills are passing into irrelevance. Yet this happens all the time, especially in business, as we'll see in the case of the Swiss watch industry (see Chapter 3).

NOTES

1. A. Grove, *Only the Paranoid Survive* (New York: Harper Collins Business, 1996).

Wishful Thinking

ook at almost any major screwup in the real world and you will find
that somewhere someone is basing a decision on what she *wants* rather
than what she *knows*. We call it "wishful thinking," and it's everywhere.

Wishful thinking is about deciding that the world is a certain way not
because we have evidence that it is that way but because it would be painful to
decide otherwise.

One way to look at wishful thinking is as optimism run amok. Optimism
is a wonderful trait. Studies show that people who are optimistic do better at
almost everything. Optimism is the basis of persistence, and persistence is the
basis of success. People who are optimistic try harder, and often they don't
stop when things go wrong. In our ancestors this was a survival trait. The
caveman who tried a few more times to catch a fish or who was certain that
eventually he could figure out a way to get the honey without the attracting
the notice of the bees tended to survive better than his more easily
discouraged neighbor.

However, like anything else, too much optimism can be a bad thing. If
you're sure there is no way to fail, you're bound to try something stupid.
Everyone who ever died trying to go over Niagara Falls in a barrel was an
optimist. Because intelligent people are better able to visualize the consequences of an action, they can be at greater risk of spending so much time
thinking about success that they can't bear to consider failure. This prevents
them from acknowledging the possibility that things might not go as
planned.

Another aspect of high intelligence that can set a person up for wishful
thinking is that smart people have often had success in life, which can get

them thinking that, one way or another, everything will always work out for the best.

The fact is that the problems faced by our ancestors were simpler than the issues we deal with today. Wishful thinking thrives in situations where the outcome is uncertain and the rewards for success are high, but it only expresses itself when the thinker has options. Today, most of our complex problems have many possible solutions; thus the wishful thinker has more scope to pick a more appealing, and more disastrous, option.

Among the characteristics we will see in the wishful thinking cases are:

- **Strong desire.** Wishful thinking starts with the wish. In all cases there is something the thinker wants: life after death, to avoid war, to become rich, not to die, and so on. This is the defining characteristic of wishful thinking. People who negotiate for a living, such as real estate agents and some lawyers, will tell you that you should never negotiate for something you want too badly. They say you won't be able to conduct the process rationally. Perhaps there is a related rule that you should never bet too much on your own thinking about something you want too badly. Wishful thinking tends to flourish in situations where there are no good choices. It is in exactly this kind of situation when we need to be wary of undue optimism.

- **Optimism.** Since optimism underlies wishful thinking, it is no surprise that many of the cases involve people with a basically optimistic worldview, or at least not a pessimistic one.

- **A perception of an "edge."** This is not present in all cases, but often wishful thinkers seem to know that they are straying from normal thought patterns. To help compensate for this, they develop a reason why their case is different. It can be because a new technology is going to make everyone rich, or because they have special influence over a dictator, but it is typically something that outsiders would recognize for the rationalization it is.

- **Previous success.** If optimism underlies wishful thinking, personal success can underlie optimism. This is the reason why wishful thinking is such a trap for smart people: They have had success, they have good intuition, things work out for them. This fact makes them vulnerable to the error of wishful thinking.

- **Avoidance of disconfirming evidence.** When evidence that doesn't support the wish appears, wishful thinkers find ways to avoid it, often by focusing only on a small slice of the data.

SCIENCE

Wishful thinking has been fairly well documented by psychologists. Most people have no trouble believing that we sometimes lose sight of reality when we dearly want something. There is also plenty of evidence for the benefits that general optimism provides in our daily lives.

A study in which researchers asked participants to look up bits of obscure data in an almanac illustrates the existence of wishful thinking.[1] The bits of information they were asked to find included such trivia as the literacy rate in Chile and the president of a particular college, things that most people are not likely to know off the top of their heads. The subjects were asked to predict how well they would be able to perform the task under three conditions: one where no reward would be given for performance, one in which a cash reward would be given based on who was able to perform the task most effectively, and one in which a cash reward would be given at random.

As long as there was nothing at stake, the subjects were fairly good at predicting how well they would do on the tasks, but when they thought they were competing for a prize, they overestimated their own capabilities significantly. Thus, the prospect of winning something seemed to interfere with the subjects' ability to predict their own performance level.

There is a twist to this experiment in which men and women were evaluated separately, and men seemed to be much more prone to this error than women. The experimenter suggested that the difference was due to the competitive nature of the task, which led the female subjects to moderate their predictions because they were less comfortable aggressively predicting success in competition than were the men; the results also suggest that there might be differences between the sexes in susceptibility to wishful thinking.

In another interesting study of wishful thinking, researchers asked students to estimate whether their own chances of experiencing certain life events were greater or less than those of their classmates.[2] The life events, both positive and negative, included such desirable goals as owning one's own home and traveling to Europe, and serious problems such as alcoholism or attempting suicide. By a striking margin the students showed "unrealistic optimism" in their responses. For some questions optimistic responses outnumbered pessimistic ones by eight or nine to one. Obviously everyone in the group couldn't be luckier than everyone else in the group, so this study constitutes a great proof for wishful thinking.

If wishful thinking is an outgrowth of general optimism, then why did evolution program us to be optimistic? Psychologist Martin Seligman has done some interesting studies on the impact that optimism can have on our ability to be effective in our daily lives. After doing pioneering work on pessimism and depression, Seligman became interested in their opposites. He and his group developed a questionnaire to assess people's level of optimism and used it to investigate the impact optimism has on our general ability to perform in day-to-day life.

In one experiment researchers administered their questionnaire to a group of insurance salesmen. They found that the salesmen who scored in the upper half of the group in optimism sold 37 percent more than those in the bottom half, and those in the top tenth sold 88 percent more than those in the bottom tenth.[3]

This is not especially surprising. Selling is a difficult profession in which sellers get a lot more rejection than acceptance. You would expect optimistic people to do much better at it than pessimists. In addition, it could be that consistent success at work makes people more optimistic rather than the other way around, so the researchers recognized that more study was needed.

The insurance company Seligman was working with was impressed with the results of his study and decided to experiment by hiring a special force of agents who would not normally have been picked based on standard staffing practices but who scored well on the optimism instrument. Two years later the average sales in this group were 27 percent greater than those hired in the normal way, indicating that optimism may be more important than any other factor in picking successful salespeople.

But salespeople have an unusual job. There is probably no profession where optimism is more important than in selling something like insurance. However, we can find similar evidence in other areas of endeavor.

The mechanism that makes optimism such a powerful positive trait was shown in another study Seligman describes. In this one the researchers gave the optimism test to a group of competitive college swimmers and followed them through their season.

At the end of the season the swimmers were each asked to swim one of their best events. When they finished, they were told that their times were disappointing, between 1.5 and 5 seconds slower than they actually were. This was shocking and disheartening for the athletes; one swimmer sat in a corner for twenty minutes and rocked like a baby, according to Seligman.

Then the swimmers were asked to repeat their events. The pessimists tended to get worse on this second trial. Apparently they were having a difficult time regaining their mental equilibrium after the disappointment of their first run. The optimists got better, some by 2 to 5 seconds. Apparently they were challenged rather than discouraged by the adversity and determined to come back as strong as possible.

This tells us something about why our optimistic ancestors tended to survive to pass their genes down to us. When confronted with a challenge or failure, pessimists crumble; optimists dig in and do better next time. In prehistoric times this was a matter of life and death, but even today, being sure that events will turn out for the better can enable us to ignore things we would rather remain unaware of, leading to errors in judgement.

CASES

Sir Arthur Conan Doyle and the Cottingly Fairies

Sir Arthur Conan Doyle (May 22, 1859—July 7, 1930) is best known today as the creator of Sherlock Holmes, that most thoughtful and logical of crime fighters. Conan Doyle published Holmes stories from 1880 to 1914, even today admirers continue to write new Holmes tales, and the old adventures continue to be read by the general public. Holmes has become part of our cultural landscape, and few of us wouldn't recognize him in his distinctive deerstalker hat. The stories were hugely popular, as eagerly awaited and read as the Harry Potter books are today.

Most people are not aware that there was another side to Doyle. An intelligent man, if not quite the equal of his fictional creation, he was also a pitiably gullible one. He wanted so passionately to believe in a happy ending to our time on earth that he was seduced by all manner of fakers and frauds who were willing to tell him that his dead nephews, son, and friends were happy in the afterlife and that he could communicate with them. He was so desperately committed to this belief that he was willing to accept the most ridiculous tales as fact.

Conan Doyle was a physically strong and mentally energetic man, and he led an interesting life. He was a war correspondent in Africa, supervised a hospital there during the Boer War, and spoke out against Belgian oppression of the Congo.

Conan Doyle was also a genuinely nice person. Harry Houdini, who was his friend, wrote that Lady Doyle told him that he had "never spoken a cross word in their marriage."[4] Even his detractors thought him a genuinely good man.

Conan Doyle was born into a Catholic family in Scotland in 1859, and while not a prodigy he was an intelligent and curious lad. An aggressive reader, he borrowed so many books from the local library that a rule was passed forbidding any patron to check out more than three books a day.

Young Conan Doyle went to Edinburgh University, receiving a doctor of medicine degree. In 1882 he opened his practice.

Times were tough at first for the young doctor, but Conan Doyle was sharp and persistent. He played on a number of local amateur sports teams, thus becoming known in the community. Eventually his practice did reasonably well.

During his time as a struggling young physician, Doyle took up writing stories and articles for magazines both to make a bit of extra money and to pass the time. He had already published a short story that he wrote while a medical student, but he did not really pursue writing until his young medical practice gave him the time and motivation. His first works were not tremendously successful, but in 1887 he published "A Study in Scarlet," the first Sherlock Holmes story. At that point his future changed. Eventually Holmes would free Conan Doyle from normal work and allow him to indulge his naturally curious nature. In addition to the Holmes stories, Conan Doyle wrote fiction, including well-regarded but not commercially successful historical novels, nonfiction, and plays.

Conan Doyle had a long-standing interest in the occult. Like any intelligent person, he had asked himself the transcendental questions: Why do we exist? and What is to finally become of us? His Catholic upbringing, which he had abandoned, did not give him the answers he needed, and for many years he dabbled in psychic research. These studies were not considered disreputable at that time, and a number of qualified researchers looked for evidence of life after death, the soul, and all manner of psychic powers. As a young doctor Conan Doyle attended séances and table-tipping (a séance in which the spirits would move the table around which the audience sat) demonstrations. He remained an interested, halfhearted believer. Eventually, however, he would become deeply involved in spiritualism.

Spiritualism was a combination of religion, occult practice, and out-and-out fraud. Like most religions, spiritualism taught that the dead still existed somewhere; spiritualism was unique, however, in that it believed the dead remained on call to communicate regularly with their living loved ones in a wide variety of ways. These methods included the kind of mediumship still practiced today in which a "sensitive" receives messages from the dead to relay to the living and a number of more bizarre practices that have become less common, such as table tipping, blowing of "spirit trumpets," and writing on slates that had been put in boxes or were otherwise supposedly kept safe from tampering by mere humans. A specialty catalog even sold a séance chair with collapsible arms to allow the medium to free his or her hands to manipulate various objects in the dark and produce effects for the séance. Spiritualism was very big for much of the last half of the 1800s.

Today this type of spirit contact is mostly restricted to teenage slumber parties and a small number of operations that prey on society's most gullible members. You can still find it in a few places like Camp Chesterfield in Indiana, which bills itself as "A Spiritual Center of Light."

Camp Chesterfield is a tawdry place. There, for a price, you can get your fortune told, speak with loved ones, or have a little trinket, cheap jewelry, or a polished stone "apported" for you, meaning materialized from the ether by a spirit. These spirits will also write messages to you and do drawings. When one of America's most accomplished psychic investigators, Joe Nickell,[5] pointed out to a woman who had just received a painting from a spirit that her picture included the telltale pattern of dots from the halftone printing process—the mediums often produce these spirit pictures the mediums by using a newspaper or magazine picture and transferring the image with solvents—she was momentarily discomfited but stated that she simply chose to believe.

Lamar Keene's book *The Psychic Mafia* details how many of these tricks are done.[6] Keene was a Chesterfield medium before coming clean in his book about the tricks used there. The phrase "chose to believe" is important here.

Many people seem to make a choice to believe in circumstances where not believing is painful. Conan Doyle was one of these people.

Spiritualism was fading in the early 1900s until World War I, when bereaved individuals desperate to get in touch with their loved ones flocked to mediums. Eventually the more bizarre and theatrical practices faded away, mostly because time and again fraudulent mediums were caught manipulating the slates with trick boxes or sleight-of-hand and tipping the séance table with their feet. Today's mediums stick mostly to relaying messages and skip the cheapest of the theatrics.

Many writers have stated that Conan Doyle got involved in spiritualism to assuage the pain of losing his son Kingsley in World War I. This is not the case. In actuality, Kingsley Conan Doyle died in 1918 of influenza contracted during the war. Conan Doyle publicly announced his belief in spiritualism in October 1917 and received the news of Kingsley's death on the way to a spiritualist speaking engagement. Conan Doyle probably became a believer in spiritualism sometime in early 1916.

That said, it's probable that Kingsley's death and that of Conan Doyle's younger brother, Innes, in 1919 deepened his commitment to the spiritualist movement. Through spiritualist mediums, he believed, he was able to communicate with his lost son, brother, mother, and other loved ones. People say that of all the tragedies that can be experienced in life, losing a child is the most terrible. Thus, we can allow Conan Doyle some sympathy as we look at his case. Certainly few of us can claim with certainty that we would do better.

Conan Doyle's great need to believe came from other sources as well. By 1917 he had seen quite a bit of death. He had served in the Boer war, and his nephew, his sister's husband, and his wife's brother all died in the Great War. Also, his first wife, Louisa, was an invalid for thirteen years with tuberculosis. Conan Doyle spent long periods by her side in sanitariums surrounded by the dying before she passed away herself in 1906. It is easy to see that a man who had suffered such losses and spent so much time facing man's ultimate fate might be unable to resist the lure of a thought system that not only holds out hope of survival after death, but claims to provide proof, and also claims that death does not have to keep a person from talking regularly to loved ones.

Conan Doyle made no bones about the relief he got from his spiritualist beliefs:

People ask, "What do you get from Spiritualism?" The first thing you get is that it absolutely removes all fear of death. Secondly, it bridges death for those dear ones whom we may love. We need have no fear that we are calling them back, for all we do is to make such conditions as experience has taught us will enable them to come if they wish, and the initiative lies always with them. They have many times told us that they would not come back if it were not God's will, and it makes them intensely happy to help and comfort us, to tell us about their happy life in that world to which we are in our turn destined to come.[7]

The evidence that finally convinced Conan Doyle of the reality of spiritualism, along with his overwhelming will to believe, came from Lily Loder-Symonds. Loder-Symonds was an old friend of the Conan Doyle's, and had been a bridesmaid at his first wedding. When Louisa's health began to fail, Loder-Symonds lived with the couple as a companion. As Louisa's health worsened, Loder-Symonds took up the practice of "automatic writing." In this method of communicating with the dead, the medium sits with a pen and paper and attempts to enter a trance in which the spirits will write through her. She was not perfect, but apparently she scored enough successes that, combined with Conan Doyle's increasing need to believe, he finally was convinced of the reality of the spiritualist worldview. He made this comment about Loder-Symonds's writing:

Of all forms of mediumship this seems to me to be the one which should be tested most rigidly, as it lends itself very easily not so much to deception as to self-deception, which is a more subtle and dangerous thing. Is the lady herself writing, or is there, as she avers, a power that controls her. . . . In the case of L. S. there is no denying that some messages proved to be not true, specially in the matter of time they were quite unreliable. But on the other hand, the numbers which did come true were far beyond what any guessing or coincidence could account for.[8]

For instance, after the sinking of the ocean liner *Lusitania,* Loder-Symonds predicted that this event "will have a great influence on the war." The torpedoing of the *Lusitania* did indeed draw the United States into the war in a way that was by no means certain at the time. While this kind of thing might be considered rather thin evidence on which to base an entire worldview, at least at this point the creator of Sherlock Holmes still seemed to be applying some logic to the subject. Certainly he was not the only person to have concluded that some people can speak with the dead.

If this seems like a fairly mild case of wishful thinking, what followed was much worse. Conan Doyle seemed to lose all ability to discriminate the possible from the absurd on the subject of spiritualism. Perhaps, having felt the soothing touch of belief, it became ever more horrible for him to think that his belief, even in small parts, might be mistaken. Certainly he was no longer interested in anything that showed or even hinted that his beliefs might have some weaknesses. He wrote:

> The objective side of it ceased to interest, for having made up one's mind that it was true there was an end of the matter. The religious side of it was clearly of infinitely greater importance.[9]

Biographers have enjoyed pointing at a segment of Conan Doyle's book *The Stark Munro Letters* in which Munro describes himself in a way that seems to have fit Conan Doyle to a T:

> I am, I think, one of the most unsuspicious men upon earth, and through a certain easy-going indolence of disposition I never even think of the possibility of those with whom I am brought into contact trying to deceive me. It does not occur to me.[10]

The problem is illustrated in the next passage, written when Conan Doyle was well entrenched in belief in spiritualism.

> Spiritual truth does not come as a culprit to a bar, but you must rather submit in a humble spirit to psychic conditions and so go forth, making most progress when on your knees.[11]

Or, in other words, you have to believe first, then you will see the evidence. And why do you believe first? Because you want to.

Conan Doyle's belief got regular support from mediums who were willing to conjure his loved ones for him. Here he describes the first time a medium conjured his son's spirit:

> We had strong phenomena from the start, and the medium was always groaning, muttering, or talking, so that there was never a doubt where he was. Suddenly I heard a voice.
>
> "Jean (Conan Doyle's second wife, Jean Lena Annette), it is I."
>
> My wife cried, "It is Kingsley."

I said, "Is that you, boy?"

He said in a very intense whisper and a tone all his own, "Father!" And then after a pause, "Forgive me!"

I said, "There was never anything to forgive, you were the best son a man ever had." A strong hand descended on my head which was slowly pressed forward, and I felt a kiss just above my brow.

"Are you Happy?" I cried.

There was a pause and then very gently, "I am so happy."[12]

We are left to wonder not just at how Conan Doyle could have fallen for such flummery, but also at the despicable nature of the individuals who perpetrated it on him.

Conan Doyle's friendship with Houdini provides some of the best evidence of his inability to distinguish truth from falsehood in the face of his great belief in spiritualism. Although Houdini was also a candidate for spiritualism, having lost his mother, to whom he was devoted and apparently wished very much to contact again, but he was well known for debunking psychics and spiritualists by revealing their methods. Eventually Houdini's revelations led to a falling out between the two men.

Houdini's medium debunking exploits were well known to Conan Doyle, who reached the bizarre conclusion that the great magician could not be escaping from locked chests underwater and other feats using mere stage magic; rather, Houdini must have paranormal powers. He wrote to Houdini:

You have driven me to the occult! I heard about your remarkable feat in Bristol. My dear chap, why go around the world seeking a demonstration of the occult when you are giving one all the time?[13]

Houdini was never able to convince Conan Doyle that he performed his tricks using normal methods of creating illusions, great dexterity, and practice rather than supernatural powers. Nor did Houdini become any less skeptical or more confident in his friends' judgment when Mrs. Conan Doyle oversaw a séance in which she claimed that Houdini's mother spoke to him through her. Unfortunately Mrs. Conan Doyle spoke in English, a language Houdini's mother did not understand, and called him Houdini rather than his given name, Eric, the name his mother would have used, if she didn't call him by his Yiddish or Hebrew name.

Conan Doyle also exhibited his will to believe in his defense of mediums who were caught cheating. Henry Slade, one of the great slate writers of the day, was a favorite of Conan Doyle's. Slade was caught cheating several times; sometimes he used a slate on which he had previously written messages and, using sleight-of-hand, concealed the writing until it was time to reveal the spirit's message to the client. In a letter to Houdini, Conan Doyle wrote that Slade was

> capable of cheating, but I am sure he did not always cheat. The Ray Lankaster (an investigator who caught Slade using pre-written slates) conviction seems to me a just one, but on the other hand his work before Zollner, Weber, Shenibner and Court Conjurer Bellachin was, I think, beyond all doubt.[14]

Most people assume that a fraud is a fraud, especially when it involves clarified cheating with sleight-of-hand which takes a certain amount of preparation and practice; it is generally not something that an otherwise honest person could decide to do on the spur of the moment to avoid disappointing a client. People who cheat during séances come prepared to cheat. And if that's the case, then how much credibility can you have?

All of the above would go far toward illustrating Conan Doyle's wishful thinking, but the more extreme examples were yet to come.

In 1917 two young girls in Yorkshire, England, Frances Griffiths, age ten, and Elsie Wright, age sixteen, borrowed Elsie's father's new camera and took pictures that showed the two of them with what appeared to be six- to eight-inch-tall fairies playing in a garden. The girls' families didn't make much of the pictures. Elsie had worked in a photographer's studio and was known to be in the habit of drawing fairies, so the pictures were excused as a youthful prank. But as time went by, Elsie's mother got involved in an occult group. Soon the pictures began to be circulated in these occult groups, eventually coming to the attention of Edward Gardner, a building contractor who was also president of the London branch of the Theosophical Society, an organization devoted to spiritual phenomena.

After Gardner began featuring the photos in his lectures, they came to the attention of Conan Doyle. Coincidentally, Conan Doyle had just written an article suggesting that fairies do indeed exist based on testimony from unimpeachable sources, such as his children, who claimed to have seen fairies themselves.

Conan Doyle apparently instantly leaned toward the belief that these were genuine photographs. He wrote to Houdini, who had asked him for some unrelated photographs:

> But I have something far more precious—Two photos, one of a goblin, the other of four fairies in a Yorkshire wood. A fake! You will say. No, sir, I think not. However, all inquiry will be made.[15]

Conan Doyle was busy with his speaking tours and left the initial investigation of the fairies to Gardner, who took the pictures to a reputed photography expert named Harold Snelling. Snelling judged the pictures to be completely genuine:

> These two negatives are entirely genuine and unfaked photographs of single exposure, open air work, show movement in all fairy figures, and there is no trace whatever of studio work involving card or paper models, dark backgrounds, painted figures, etc. In my opinion they are both straight, untouched figures.[16]

Conan Doyle had experts at Kodak, a leading camera maker, look at the pictures also and was told that although they did not appear to be double exposures, the company could not duplicate the pictures themselves and thus could not certify the fairies as genuine. Eventually the girls produced three more pictures, all of which Conan Doyle accepted as real.

This was all it took to convince Conan Doyle that the fairies were genuine, and he immediately wrote a book about it. *The Coming of the Fairies* was published in 1922. It was the end of his credibility with the mainstream. The newspapers had a field day with him, as can be imagined.

To the modern eye, the pictures are obvious fakes. The fairies are paper cutouts and absurdly dressed in the latest fashions and hairstyles of the era. They have been identified as coming from a popular children's book, *Princess Mary's Gift Book,* which included the poem "A Spell for a Fairy" by Alfred Noyes that gave instructions for summoning the little people. Apparently Elsie decided that the magic was beyond her and fell back on her own skills at drawing, a less romantic but probably more reliable method of fairy conjuration.

In 1982 the girls finally came clean and admitted that the fairies were cutout drawings. Frances stated that "from where I was, I could see the hatpins holding up the figures. I've always marveled that anybody ever took it seriously."[17]

Elsie wrote that the girls "felt sad" for Conan Doyle:

> He had just lost his son in the war, and I think the poor man was trying to comfort himself in these things, so I said to Frances, "we are a lot younger than Conan Doyle and Mr. Gardner, so we will wait till they die of old age and then we will tell."[18]

Gardner lived to be 100 so the secret remained hidden for some time. A friend of the family suggested that Gardner and Conan Doyle were simply too important to be told by two young girls that they were wrong.

Why did Conan Doyle buy into such an egregious fake? I think Elsie got a lot of it right. He wanted, *needed* to believe. If fairies could exist, then spiritualism could be true. He also hoped that the proof of existence of fairies would help the spiritualist cause:

> The recognition of their existence will jolt the material twentieth century mind out of its heavy ruts in the mud, and will make it admit that there is a glamour and mystery to life. Having discovered this, the world will not find it so difficult to accept that spiritual message, supported by physical facts, which has already been put before it.[19]

This may be his worst bit of wishful thinking of all: How could anyone think that people would take to the notion of fairies based on a set of photographs? Probably Conan Doyle also needed to believe in the fairies because they represented another paranormal phenomenon that was out of step with current thought. If fairies truly did not exist, it would mean the skeptics were right, which would imply that they might be right in challenging spiritualism, which Conan Doyle could not abide. Conan Doyle would believe in almost any paranormal phenomenon, simply because he hoped that if they were all true, then the reality of spiritualism was beyond doubt.

In addition, Conan Doyle did not believe that children lie. He saw children, girls especially, as pure creatures, which makes one wonder how much of a hand he took in raising his own children. Anyone who has spent much time with them knows that children are the most prolific, if not the most sophisticated, liars in the human race.

Conan Doyle was also a great believer in spirit photography, which may have disposed him to take the pictures at face value. He had a large collection of photographs purporting to include the faces of the dead. Allegedly the dead are capable of showing themselves on photographs when desired, an irresistible draw for someone who had lost a loved one. Unfortunately, some of Conan Doyle's pictures also included the faces of living football players and the American boxer "Battling Siki." They were simple double exposures, a process that is well-known today but uncommon at the time.

Overall, however, it is fairly clear that the worst excesses of Conan Doyle's gullibility were brought on by his burning need to believe that arose from the deaths he and his nation had experienced and his abiding need for death not to be the end.

The case of Conan Doyle illustrates two common features of wishful thinking:

1. There is something that the thinker wants so badly that it is painful to contemplate not having it.

2. The thinker seeks the company of like-minded believers, as Conan Doyle did by spending so much of his time with other spiritualists at conventions and speaking engagements.

Financial Euphoria

There is probably no higher level of wishful thinking than that attained by someone who has a hot tip on the stock market and is convinced that this is the scheme that is going to set her up for life. This is especially true when it appears that others no more intelligent than she are making fabulous amounts of money.

The term "financial euphoria" refers to the condition when large numbers of people are afflicted with this get-rich-quick disease at the same time. Financial euphoria is not wholly the product of wishful thinking; there is an element of tribal thought in it as well, which we will look at in Chapter 4. But it is such a perfect example of the impact that hope can have on the reasoning ability of smart people that it fits better here than elsewhere.

In terms of financial euphoria, Americans today are probably most familiar with the dot.com run-up of the 1990s, when valuations for any company with a business plan including the words "e-commerce," even if on the back of a tequila-soaked bar rag, skyrocketed to dozens of times what any rational analysis would allow. During this period anyone suggesting that these valuations were not sustainable was told that they "didn't get it" and that such "old economy" ideas as cash flow and profit were no longer required for business success.

The chickens, as they always do, came home to roost eventually and set things straight, but there was plenty of pain and anguish in the adjustment.

The best book on the subject of financial euphoria is economist John Kenneth Galbraith's *A Short History of Financial Euphoria*.[20] Galbraith provides examples of this phenomenon, including the great Stock Market Crash of 1929, the Florida real estate boom of 1924 to 1926 (the phrase "If you believe that I've got some swampland in Florida to sell you" has its genesis in this debacle), and the 1987 market crash, which Galbraith predicted. Galbraith suggests that these episodes are predicable and occur on a twenty-year or so cycle. Just long enough for the next generation of financial whiz kids to grow up ignorant of the fate of their predecessors.

Commercial organizations are more vulnerable to wishful thinking than to some other kinds of errors in this book. This is because wishful thinking is a forward-looking mistake, and the one great reality check of the commercial world, financial performance, doesn't really kick in until after the damage is done. In addition, optimism is a highly desired quality in executives, as we saw earlier, and the successful ones sometimes develop more of it as their careers progress and they have one success after another.

In general, episodes of financial euphoria have at their core a belief that something new has been found under the financial sun and that those who get in on it have almost unlimited prospects for gain. This can be anything from Florida real estate to junk bonds. As Galbraith points out, however, the business of finance does not often spawn anything truly new. Most of the big new things people think they find amount to a twist on the idea of "leverage"; that is, securing large amounts of money with relatively small real assets.

Financial euphoria is created when the price of an asset, such as a stock, ceases to be driven by any calculation of its worth and begins to stem from the fact that people believe that it will continue to rise, regardless of any real appreciation in value.

The classic case of financial euphoria was the Dutch tulip craze, or Tulipomania, of the 1630s, during which investors beggared themselves for tulip bulbs, secure in the knowledge that they could never depreciate—until, that is, they did. This incident has been written about extensively, so instead we'll look at a less well known but just as interesting debacle: the South Sea bubble.

South Sea Bubble

Since this book is about smart people doing stupid things, the South Sea bubble is a great example since no less an intellect than Sir Isaac Newton, one of humanity's greatest thinkers, lost over $1 million (in today's money) in stock speculation in this period. He actually sold his stock in the South Sea Company, but as its price continued to rise, he was unable to resist buying back in and got caught in the inevitable crash.

The South Sea Company was founded in 1711. England at that time had a huge debt, much of which had been incurred in the War of the Spanish Succession. A group of merchants holding about £9 million worth of government bonds were given the opportunity to exchange those bonds for stock in the company in return for interest payments and a monopoly on trade to the South Seas. Basically, the "South Seas" was the term used for that part of the Americas controlled by Spain, but especially the west coasts of Central and South America, where untold riches were believed to be. The treaty ending the war was expected to provide Britain some favorable trade arrangements in the New World.

Unfortunately, nobody told the Spaniards about this aspect of the treaty, and Philip V of Spain was having none of it. He granted the English a contract to supply slaves to his colonies and allowed them a single trade voyage a year, with over 20 percent of the profits going to him.

Although the South Sea Company was never especially successful, its stock remained highly regarded, and in 1720 it proposed to take on the entire national debt of England—about £31 million—again offering its own stock in trade for the government bonds. The transaction was rather complex, but basically the company was authorized to issue 315,000 shares of stock at a nominal value of £100 each. These shares were given to the holders of the government debt, who made a profit in the exchange and also received a tradable instrument instead of just government debt. If the stock could be sold at more than £100 per share, then less of it would have to be used to cover the debt, leaving profit for the existing shareholders, many of whom were in management or otherwise important men in the government.

The only speaker against the scheme in the House of Commons was Robert Walpole, who said:

> The great principle of the project was an evil of first-rate magnitude; it was to raise artificially the value of the stock, by exciting and keeping up a

general infatuation, and by promising dividends out of funds which could never be adequate to the purpose.[21]

This apt characterization also applies to the tactics of a number of dot.coms 230 years later, when wishful thinking was encouraged to pump up a stock. Walpole did not find a willing audience for his cautions.

As in the dot.com fiasco, the directors of the South Sea Company and their friends employed every means they could find to run up the stock price before the exchange was made. Rumors circulated about pending treaties with Spain that would allow the company to trade without restraint, and the precious metal mines of the New World were talked up until it seemed that all England would be awash in silver. The scheme sailed through the House of Commons.

The members of the company's board and several influential members of Parliament received sizable blocks of stock, which helped to convince the average investor that the stock was a good thing not to be missed out on. The stock rose rapidly in price, from £128.5 in January 1720, to £300 in April right after the bill passed, to £1,000 in August. The nation was simply crazed for stock in the company. Thinking that the stock appreciation reflected their own financial acumen in purchasing it, the newly rich rushed to purchase more.

Much of this stock run-up was the work of the company directors, led by John Blunt, the Baptist son of a shoemaker, who worked under the belief that the best thing for the company was whatever advanced its stock price. In some ways this is the same attitude that has contributed to spectacular failures in the modern era, Enron being only a single example. In the case of the South Sea Company, the stock price was bolstered by such mechanisms as selling shares for only 20 percent down and making loans to stockholders against the value of their stock to make it more attractive.

The joint-stock company, one owned by stockholders, had been around for years, but this episode served to place it prominently in the public eye. The normal cadre of criminals, cads, and rakes watched this happen with great interest. If the directors of the South Sea Company could get rich this way, why couldn't everyone? There was an orgy of joint-stock offerings for every conceivable scheme, including a machine gun, a boat designed to bring live fish to London markets, a firm to obtain saltpeter by emptying every lavatory in England, and a perpetual motion machine. All of these, however, take a backseat to the most audacious scheme of all, advertised as "a company for carrying on an undertaking of great advantage, but nobody to know what it is."[22]

One almost wants to shake the hand of the rotter who came up with this one, if only for his audacity. He offered 5,000 shares at £100 each, which could be bought for a deposit of £2. Every share would entitle the owner to £100 every year forever, although it was never explained how this money was to be obtained. The author of this scheme opened his office at 9:00 in the morning and by 3:00 had taken deposits on 1,000 shares. He must then have reevaluated his capital requirements and found that they were not as great as he had thought. He was never seen again. His subscribers were not stupid; they were in the grip of wishful thinking. (Okay, in this case at least some of them were stupid.)

Enough people saw the danger in this situation that in June 1720, three months before South Sea Company crashed, these joint-stock companies were declared a public nuisance and outlawed. Apparently the the directors of the South Sea Company, who disliked competition for the capital of the unwary, had a role in the law's passage.

All London was engulfed in stock speculation, but the South Sea Company remained the center of it. In July the *Mercure Historique et Politique* reported:

> The South Sea Company is continually a source of wonderment. The sole topic of conversation in England revolves around the shares of this Company, which have produced vast fortunes for many people in such a short space of time. Moreover it is to be noted that trade had completely slowed down, that more than one hundred ships moored along the river Thames are for sale, and that the owners of capital prefer to speculate on shares than to work at their normal business.[23]

In this passage we see foreshadowing of the big tech stock run-up of the 1990s, in which so many people found themselves millionaires, retired, and were later forced back to work when the market fell. Clearly the whole country was in the grip of a shared wishful euphoria that left many otherwise sensible people without the basic ability to judge risk.

In June 1720, despite the directors' best efforts, the lack of real value behind the company began to tell and the stock fell into the 800s. By buying aggressively, the directors were able to stop the fall at about 750 and even push share prices back up to 1,000, but they immediately started falling again, especially as people found out that several highly placed directors, including the chairman, John Blunt, had sold out. Share prices continued to fall throughout August, reaching around 700 at the beginning of September.

Then the bubble burst. The stock went into free fall and ended the month around 200. The Sword Blade Bank, the company's bank, which had issued many loans using South Sea stock as collateral, failed first, but others followed and thousands of investors were ruined. Eventually the directors' manipulations became public. Some tried to flee to the Continent; others chose to stay and try to talk their way out of it, but it was too late. The directors had become scapegoats, albeit deservedly. Many were imprisoned and reduced to near beggary as their estates were confiscated for their roles in the fiasco.

While the directors got their deserved comeuppance, the public played the role of the wounded innocent rather than that of the greedy fool. This is something of a pattern in these cases: The leaders are punished but those who contribute to their own destruction with their greed and ignorance seldom admit their role.

Four characteristics of wishful thinking are visible in the South Sea Company case.

1. There is something that looks new. This convinces people that the old rules do not apply. In this case it was the joint-stock company, which was not actually new but had not had this kind of exposure before. Wishful thinking cases often include the belief that the thinker has an "edge" that will make his or her experience different from that of other people.

2. Insiders manipulated the price of stock in the South Sea Company in ways that we would call criminal today, but which still go on, especially with the Internet available as a nearly anonymous venue for pumping up a stock. People chose to believe this information despite the untrustworthy nature of its source.

3. The wishful thinkers ignored overwhelming evidence that the world was not as they wanted it to be and attacked those who presented that evidence to them.

4. Most important, there is an overwhelming will to believe. Eventually, not believing causes the victim so much pain that it becomes unbearable and he believes simply to ease his own anxiety.

Dot.Com Crash: Value America

The Internet economy has been the South Sea bubble of the later twentieth century, complete with wishful thinking, ventures to make a lot of money but nobody knowing how, illicit stock pumping, and a huge crash at the end. In the final crash, the Internet economy lost over 100,000 jobs, with hundreds of companies closing their doors.

The examples of wishful thinking in this disaster are many. iHarvest.com spent $7 million trying to sell a service people could use to store Web pages and addresses, apparently not knowing that the most common Internet browsers had buttons to do this already. Calendarcentral.com tried to sell a service providing shared calendars, which duplicated Microsoft products Outlook and Exchange. IAM.com burned up $50 million putting together a database of aspiring actors to take the place of talent agencies, apparently not realizing that talent agencies serve a purpose and that directors really do like having someone prescreen budding stars for them, rather than looking at a million headshots, which all look alike. Officeclick.com ran a Web site targeting secretaries and threw away $35 million before someone realized that: (1) nobody wants to advertise to secretaries, and (2) secretaries don't have time to screw around on the Web at work. Zing.com destroyed $14 million trying to get people to download a piece of software that would let them look at advertisements while waiting for Web pages to come up. Something everybody wants to do. And finally, my two favorites, Digiscents, which wanted to make a box that would emit a smell when triggered by your computer, thus scent-enabling the Web, and last, PNV.com, which billed itself thusly:

> PNV is the leading provider of bundled telecommunications, cable television and Internet access services to truck drivers in the privacy and convenience of their truck cabs.

I can only quote industry watcher Philip Kaplan on this one, who said:

> GET YOUR EYES ON THE ROAD AND YOUR HANDS BACK ON THE GODDAM WHEEL YOU METH-ADDLED PORN ADDICTS.
>
> Look, I'm all for Internet access, but NOT WHILE YOU'RE DRIVING 80,000 POUNDS OF RIG OVER MY CAR.[24]

Another eye-popping example is Priceline.com, which went public in March 1998 and had an initial valuation of over $10 billion (yes, with a "b").

It operated a Web site where people could name their own price for airline tickets. This initial valuation was more than the current value of United Airlines, Continental Airlines, and Northwest Airlines combined, and the company had never made a dime. In 1998 it lost over $114 million. At one point it had a market capitalization greater than the entire rest of the airline industry, and two years later, with the stock at a bit over 1 percent of its high, it was worth a couple of airplanes.

There were all kinds of reasons why these companies went under. Some had a neat idea that nobody would pay for; others fell for the popular fiction that if you just got people coming to your site, you could then find a way to make money. A lot of these people banked on the idea that eventually someone would pay them to advertise on their sites, but as it turns out Web advertising is pretty ineffective, and forty to fifty times as expensive as print advertising per page view.

A number of dot.com leaders ran their companies with no spending discipline, doing things like renting Ellis Island for parties and hiring 200 people when they could have done the work with 40, just because they wanted to feel like big cheeses. A number of these concerns were run by greedy bastards who never had any intention of building a business that would create value in the world; they were just trying to keep the scam alive until the IPO (the initial public offering of the company's stock, which would presumably make them rich), and then split for the beach.

It was fairly irritating to listen to these wipeouts cry about how they were done in by "market conditions" or lecture gravely (as gravely as you can get when your first whisker is still in your future, I suppose) about how they were going to "adjust their business model moving forward." These guys were clearly thinking wishfully, but in some ways you can't blame them: a bunch of other twenty-somethings were making fortunes, and they felt entitled to one of their own.

Whatever the reasons for the crash of each company, there is the question of why investors gave company owners so much money to play with. Why did reasonably smart investors fund such silly ideas?

One reason was the "edge." Investors thought that they were in a new world, one in which traditional ways of valuing a company did not apply. They thought that the Internet had changed everything, rather like people thought the joint-stock company had changed everything in the South Sea case.

There were other problems also. The business press did an abominable job of separating the garbage from reality, and financial firms had horrible conflicts of interest and often issued misleading recommendations. But at bottom this bubble had the same causes as the others: greed and wishful thinking.

The dot.com mania matches the South Sea bubble and tulip mania in terms of irrationality. There is probably no better illustration of wishful thinking and the ills of the dot.com crash of 1999 and 2000 than Value America and its cofounder Steve Winn. A *Business Week* article from May 2000 captures the situation perfectly:

> Value America's rise and fall is emblematic of an era of unbridled optimism and outright greed. Possibly only during a period of unprecedented valuations and a seeming suspension of the rules of finance could someone of Winn's background amass the following and the finances to get a company off the ground as quickly as Value America took flight. For most of his stint at the company, Winn, who collected a salary of $295,000 a year, had little of his own money at risk. His business experience consisted mainly of leading another public company into bankruptcy. His technology experience: nil. Winn and his company practiced New Economy values with a vengeance. A massive ad budget was spent well in advance of any profits. Yawning losses were excused as a necessary evil in the pursuit of market share. There was a rush to take an untried company public at the height of the investor frenzy for new dot-com stocks.[25]

Value America was founded by Steve Winn and Rex Scatena in 1996. It was to be the archetypical Internet company. When it went public in 1999, its initial offering price of $23 per share immediately went to $74.25 before drifting back to $55. It was a $2.4 billion company that had never made a penny. By August 2000, seventeen months later, it was essentially worthless.

Value America was to be the Wal-Mart of the Net, and an "inventoryless" company. It was to be the Internet front-end and would take orders from customers, who would appreciate having a single place to go to buy everything from toothbrushes to computers, and forward those orders to manufacturers, which would fill them, thus cutting out the middlemen of distribution and traditional retailing.

There are actually two levels of wishful thinking in this case.

1. The managers and founders of Value America were thinking wishfully when they believed that the business model made sense

and that the company would eventually succeed, despite evidence to the contrary.

2. More important was the wishful thinking of the investing public. They supported a guy with Winn's history and never, ever looked more than skin deep at the operation, which was obviously ill run from early on.

Winn joined his father's housewares business after spending a tough year as a manufacturer's rep after leaving school. The business did well. Winn bought his father out and in 1986 founded Dynast Classics Corp. to make lighting products. In 1990 he took the company public, and within the year it had lost over three quarters of its value. In 1993 Dynast filed for bankruptcy.

Winn was essentially a salesman, a job for which optimism is a prerequisite, and he had all the buzzwords of the new economy down pat. Value America was to be "alliances of consumption with alliances of production" and "friction-free capitalism." The pitch was perfect for the time, but the execution was amateurish.

Winn and company were caught up in one of the myths of the Net: that profit doesn't matter. The idea was that you first had to get people coming to your Web site, then you had to make it "sticky," so that people would keep coming back. Then, once you had won the "rush for eyeballs," you could think about how to make money. If this sounds like an overstatement, I assure you that this was exactly the thought process people were buying into. What it did was let them dodge the hard question of how anyone was going to make money in the consumer Internet world, a question that is still a problem for everyone except the makers of porn. The solution was to spend a fortune on advertising for companies that had never made any money and didn't even quite know what they were selling.

But Value America bought into this idea in a big way; it spent $69 million on advertising in 1999 but got little for its money. For instance, it paid Yahoo $4.5 million for ads that brought in less than $100,000 in revenue. Value America's customer acquisition costs were at least equal to those of any "old economy" retailer.

The company's founders and board were so far caught in the grip of their wish that they felt money would never be a problem. They spent $5 million for a parcel of land on which to build a new multimillion-dollar headquarters, only to find out that the land was appraised at $2 million. This was fairly typical dot.com wastage. These guys were so sure that nothing could go wrong and that they were already titans of industry that they spent money as if they had no limits.

If the aim was to grow the company, Winn and company succeeded, but they never found a way to make money. In 1996 they lost over $400,000, about $2 million in 1997 (on sales of $134,000), $64.8 million in 1998 (on sales of $42.3 million), and a whopping $143 million in 1999. The problem was that the company was so focused on getting customers that it ignored everything else. Margins were kept very low, about 6 percent, compared to 12 percent at Costco and 23 percent at Wal-Mart, but they still were not the lowest on the Net in the most important product areas. That honor went to buy.com, and thus Value America couldn't compete on price. With a huge advertising budget on top of this, it is easy to see how the company lost money. The business model didn't pan out either. Manufacturers were not able to ship a single can of soup at a time. Glenda Dorchak, who would become CEO of Value America when all hope was gone, once tried to buy two toothbrushes from the company. The package arrived weeks later with one missing. The dirty secret behind Value America was that most orders were handled by old-economy distributors, not the highly tuned information machine that was to have had the manufacturers ship directly to the customer.

Even the technology wasn't in place. The Web site was slow, many orders were placed with distributors via fax rather than on a spiffy new computer system, and much of the company's revenue came from customers calling in on the telephone. One insider said:

> We needed to do X amount of business this quarter and add X number of products to the site so the stock price would stay high and we would all be millionaires. Who cared that the store ran like molasses or that order tracking was virtually unmanageable.[26]

Dorchak stated that "it's like icing a cake that hasn't been baked. We had someone here who was just icing an unbaked cake."[27]

Another section from the *Business Week* article shows how Winn played to the wish to keep employees motivated:

> Value America began to operate less like a business and more like a cult. "When you're around him, [Winn] you get caught in the swirl," says one former manager. "It's like drinking Kool-Aid." Winn would gather his

employees and speak for a full hour at a time, promising that everyone standing before him would someday be a millionaire.[28]

One would think that, seeing that there was no money coming in, and no immediate way to change this, the company would have scaled back, but the wish was too strong, and nothing changed until it was too late. Finally, aghast at the losses, the board fired Winn and installed Dorchak as CEO in late 1999. By August 2000 the company quit trying to do business on the net, declared bankruptcy, and tried to set itself up to provide e-business services to other retailers.

In another time, the vision of an online, inventoryless superstore might have worked, but it was executed so poorly that it never had a chance. The biggest and clearest hole in the business plan was that the manufacturers were not ready to ship ones and twos of things they made. In addition, Value America itself was not ready, it bought into the hype far too heavily, and basically nobody knew how to run it.

The basis for wishful thinking is a great desire for something, and a perceived edge in getting it. In this case the edge was Internet technology, which was going to make everyone wealthy. People bought in, and when prices rose they bought some more, until the house fell under its own weight.

It is interesting that there are still believers, even after the destruction of billions of dollars in value. Paul Allen, one of the founders of Microsoft, who was an early investor in Value America and whose name lent credibility to the fiasco, lost around $50 million. Journalist Chris Nerney reported seeing this comment on an Internet message board: "The new business model of VUSA sounds promising. Could anyone say when and how trading on VUSA will resume!"[29]

Good luck to you!

We should note for the sake of completeness that the dot.com bubble and others like it are not purely wishful thinking phenomena. A strong follow-the-herd mentality also runs through financial disasters such as these, something we will take up in Chapter 4. In this case the investing public put tremendous pressure on the managers of investment funds to do at least as well as everyone else. These individuals were well aware that if other funds continually outperformed theirs they could be looking for new jobs pretty quickly. Even if you are pretty sure the bubble is going to pop, the best thing to do is what everyone else is doing. If it works, you look good, and if it doesn't, you don't look any dumber than the next fund manager.

Of course, the larger wishful fiasco was the dot.com bubble itself. The Internet is a legitimate new technology and allows us to do things we couldn't before. But it was horribly overhyped. It was called "world changing" and "transformative" (a word employed only by academics and people trying to sell something). It was supposed to be the biggest change since the invention of agriculture.

Now, agriculture *was* a real world-changing breakthrough. You could add to that a few other discoveries, such as the germ theory of disease and the mass production techniques of the Industrial Revolution. It's a short list. At least so far the Internet is not in that league. Perhaps it will be someday, but today it isn't even close. But if you wish hard enough, you can convince yourself.

We can wish for a positive outcome, like becoming millionaires, or we can wish to avoid a negative outcome. The next case illustrates how wishful thinking can allow us to avoid admitting a painful truth until it is too late to remedy it.

Appeasement of Nazi Germany

Webster's dictionary defines appeasement as "the policy of giving in to the demands of a hostile or dangerous power in an attempt to prevent trouble."[30] The study of appeasement as a tool of statecraft is rife with political ax grinding. Politicians are quick to accuse rivals of appeasement whenever a concession is made to a rival nation. Some scholars have sought to rehabilitate the practice by defining any conciliatory move as appeasement and pointing out that in some circumstances, such an action can be effective, as when Britain made a series of minor concessions to the United States between 1896 and 1903.

What we will be looking at is a darker version of appeasement, one in which terrified leaders refuse to acknowledge the possibility of war even when faced with an enemy that is clearly willing to be the aggressor and obviously preparing for conflict. It is easy to see the wishful thinking here; the will to believe that there is an alternative to war can be overwhelming. And it is impossible to argue that this is a mistake, as far as it goes. The mistake is in refusing to acknowledge and prepare for the possibility of war even as one works for peace.

The defining instance of the failure of appeasement in modern history is Neville Chamberlain's policy toward Germany in the late 1930s. Frankly, much of the popular wisdom on this subject is wrong. While Chamberlain was not especially likable, and had a tendency to hold those who disagreed with him in contempt, he was not a hand-wringing peacenik or an ignoramus without knowledge of international affairs. Neither was he completely fooled by Hitler, despite making some rather naive comments about the dictator's trustworthiness. Chamberlain was a smart man, and in another age he might have been a fine prime minister, perhaps even a great one. He had served as Chancellor of the Exchequer from 1931 to 1937 and guided Britain through the Depression with reasonable skill. But he had a great "will to believe" that war could be averted, and he could not shake free of it when the time came. It is interesting that on some level he seemed to understand the reality of the situation but was unable to act on it. As early as 1934 he wrote in his diary: "Force is the only thing Germans understand. . . . What does not satisfy me is that we do not shape our foreign policy accordingly."[31]

Apparently even at this early date he had some understanding of Hitler's Germany, but his later actions were completely at variance with this understanding. Deep down Chamberlain believed that war "wins nothing, cures nothing, ends nothing," and so he saw no reason to participate in it.

Chamberlain was a product of his time. He had watched Britain suffer through the agonies of World War I, which had scourged Europe with devastation unlike anything it had seen previously. The pain of this loss was made even worse by the perception that the war could have been avoided if everyone involved had bargained in good faith and kept cool heads. This desire to avoid war was so strong that it began to interfere with the way Chamberlain, and many others, thought. Historian Stephan Rock phrased it this way:

> The reason . . . appears in retrospect quite simple: the policy of the British government was dominated by Wishful Thinking. There was, in fact an almost astonishing discrepancy between what British leaders increasingly came to know in their minds—that Germany could not be appeased— and what they continued to hope in their hearts—that it could.[32]

The roots of World War II and of the policy of appeasement lie in the Treaty of Versailles that ended World War I. Two provisions of the treaty were most problematic: First, much of the territory Germany lost was filled with

German-speaking people who would have preferred to remain part of their mother country. In later years when Hitler demanded the return of these territories, it was difficult for right-thinking western statesmen to oppose self-determination for the people there.

Also, Germany was forced to pay substantial reparations for the damage caused by the war. These payments hobbled the German economy and provided a flash point of discontent that allowed demagogues like Hitler to gain the attention of an embittered German populace.

Hitler himself should not have been as much of an enigma as he apparently was to Chamberlain. Hitler was convinced that Germany had lost the Great War not through being defeated on the battlefield, but because traitors within the government had capitulated to the enemy. In 1923 he and a band of followers had marched from a beer hall (thus the incident has been called the Beer Hall Putsch) to the War Ministry building in Munich, believing that the armed forces would rise to support them. He and his group were stopped by police, and Hitler was sentenced to five years in prison. This attempted putsch made it clear that he was an ideologue and prone to violence.

While in prison Hitler wrote *Mein Kampf,* in which he laid out his vision of an Aryan state. According to Hitler, when a nation needed more territory and resources, it was fully justified in taking them by force from others. Although the book was available in English translation, Chamberlain and most of his officers did not read it; thus they tended to underestimate the man's designs on Europe.

This is the first great mistake Chamberlain made in thinking about Germany and Hitler. Initially, Chamberlain believed that Hitler wanted only the return of territories lost in the Great War and self-determination for people living in those lands. In reality, Hitler wanted to make Germany supreme in Europe. And while he rarely spoke of it, data indicate that he had worldwide ambitions as well. Hitler believed in autarky, or economic self-sufficiency. He believed that Germany could not be fully secure while dependent on trade and outside powers for any essentials, be they oil, food, or anything else. Because of this viewpoint, eventually Hitler had to conquer large areas of Eastern Europe to supply food and oil for Germany. It also meant that he wanted to make Germany invulnerable to the powerful British Navy, which could only damage him through a blockade.

Hitler became chancellor of Germany in January 1933 and immediately withdrew his nation from ongoing talks on disarmament. By 1934 the

British had identified Germany as the most likely principal foe in a future major war.

In March 1935 Hitler announced that Germany would build an air force, introduce conscription, and build an army much larger than allowed by the Treaty of Versailles. In 1936 German troops were reintroduced into the previously demilitarized Rhineland. German factories built over 5,000 airplanes compared to fewer than 2,000 for Britain—a key number that should have raised eyebrows in London. Even if the British didn't know the precise numbers, the saw the general level of activity.

Chamberlain became prime minister on November 28, 1937. He succeeded the ineffective Stanley Baldwin but continued Baldwin's policy of nonconfrontation with the Germans.

In late 1937 and early 1938 attempts were made by diplomats to exchange the return of Germany's colonies for promises to behave itself in Europe. Hitler, having none of it, furthermore stated that:

> Concerning Central Europe, it should be noted that Germany would not tolerate any interference by third powers in the settlement of her relations with kindred countries or with countries having large German elements in their population.[33]

Hitler was as good as his word in this case; on March 12, 1938, Germany annexed Austria. This reintegration of a German-speaking population into Germany proper was not strongly opposed by the other European powers. But it was another sign that Hitler was not to be reasoned with.

Nevertheless, on September 6, 1938, Chamberlain wrote: "I have a feeling that things have gone in such a way as to make it more and more difficult for him to use force."[34]

After the annexation of Austria, Hitler's next target was Czechoslovakia. There was some justice in his assertions that a large number of Germans in Czech Sudetenland would have preferred to be part of Germany, although his wilder claims of widespread oppression of the Sudeten Germans were probably overblown. Hitler announced that one way or another, the Sudeten German problem would be solved to his satisfaction by October 1, 1938, setting off a diplomatic scramble to find ways to appease or at least delay the dictator.

Chamberlain took the lead in a series of meetings culminating at Munich on September 30 in which it was agreed, among the Germans, British, and

French, that Hitler could have the Sudeten Germans in return for assurances that this was all he desired and his agreement to wait until October 10 to move into the area. At the Munich Conference Hitler stated: "I don't want any Czechs. If you offered me the lot, I wouldn't accept a single one."[35]

The Czechs did not trust the German dictator, but faced with pressure from all of their possible allies and the prospect of opposing a German invasion alone, they finally agreed to pull out of the Sudetenland.

Munich was hailed as a diplomatic triumph. Chamberlain stated that we might now have "peace in our time" and was almost universally hailed as a wise and subtle statesman who had tamed the Nazis for good without spilling a drop of blood. Chamberlain himself seemed confident that the deal would hold. After Munich he recorded in his private papers that "I got the impression that here was a man who could be relied upon when he had given his word."[36]

If Chamberlain had hoped that Munich would put an end to Hitler's aggressive behavior, he was quickly disappointed. On December 10 Germany notified Britain that it was going to triple the size of its submarine fleet. At this point the British should have had no doubt about Hitler's intentions. The only target for a German U-boat fleet was England. During this time Hitler's speeches became increasingly aggressive. He talked about how Germany would gain its due by whatever means was necessary, stated that Germany had had enough interference in its affairs (his take on the Munich treaty), and insulted Chamberlain personally. At this point it was obvious that Hitler would not be appeased. Up until this time a good case could be made for most of Chamberlain's actions, and many observers have stated that it was not until Hitler invaded Czechoslovakia that his true motives were fully revealed. But a prudent statesman would at this point have had to acknowledge the probability of war and move toward what the powerful conservative Anthony Eden was calling for in Parliament: "A national effort in the sphere of defense very much greater than anything that has been attempted hitherto."[37]

While Chamberlain was disheartened, these events had no impact on his policy. He remained optimistic and in February 1939 stated: "All the information I get seems to point in the direction of peace . . . we have at last got on top of the dictators."[38]

This, at a time when it was clear to the most casual observer that, militarily at least, the allies were nowhere near being "on top of the dictators."

One aspect of Chamberlain's attitude that is interesting is his belief that he had a special ability to influence Hitler. On various occasions he stated that Hitler had been "favorably impressed" with him and that he had "won his good will" and "established influence over" him.[39] This is the I-have-an-edge aspect of wishful thinking that we have seen before and will see again. In cases of political appeasement, this wishful belief in an edge can convince the appeasing statesman of his own special powers over the aggressor.

On March 9 Chamberlain told a group of reporters that things continued to improve. He mentioned that he hoped to have a disarmament conference by the end of the year that would include the Germans. Five days later Germany invaded Czechoslovakia. Why this was such a shock is a mystery. British intelligence had provided excellent data on Hitler's plans weeks in advance, but it had been ignored.

Perhaps Hitler reconsidered whether he really wanted any Czechs. Or perhaps he just couldn't resist the bargain of picking up about 800,000 of them on the cheap. On March 14, 1939, German troops invaded Czechoslovakia and took the capital of Prague. Even then Chamberlain preferred to look for help from blind luck rather than focus on the coming war. He wrote about the possibility of issuing an ultimatum to Germany regarding Czechoslovakia and mentioned the possibility of Hitler's death:

> Our ultimatum would therefore mean war and I would never be responsible for presenting it. We shall just have to go on . . . in the hope that something would happen to break the spell, either Hitler's death or a realization that the defense was too strong to make attack feasible.[40]

The idea that Hitler might just die—he was only fifty in 1939—and save everyone a lot of trouble crops up a few times in Chamberlain's reasoning and is a great example of the wishful aspect of his thinking. It is a maybe-we'll-just-get-lucky hope with no real reason to think it might come true.

Even after this bold-faced demonstration of Nazi intentions, Britain continued to provide economic concessions to the Germans through August of that year.

Up until this time Chamberlain had done almost nothing to strengthen Britain's armed forces. A few escort ships had been built and a few fighter planes added to the Royal Air Force, but otherwise all Hitler's bellicose rhetoric, his writings in *Mein Kampf*, his massive rearmament program, his annexing of Austria, and his unreasonable demands regarding Czechoslovakia had not convinced Chamberlain to rearm Britain. This issue of rearmament was Chamberlain's third wishful blunder in dealing with Hitler. His logic ran as follows: Britain is supreme on the sea and, in a war, would eventually be able to starve and bankrupt Germany with a protracted blockade. Germany's only chance for victory was to strike quickly at the British Isles, and this could be done only by sea or air. Since the oceans were already secure, Britain only had to make itself secure in the air to be sure of eventually winning a war with Germany, especially with France fighting the German Army on the continent and further draining its resources. That said, this war would be long and arduous and might destroy both nations.

To this end, Chamberlain focused on building up his air forces, particularly his fighters, since bombers were an offensive weapon and would do little to protect the homeland but might antagonize Germany if too much emphasis were placed on them. He also resisted, until the end, any strengthening of the army.

In 1936 Duff Cooper, then secretary of war, and the army general staff had asked for seventeen army divisions that could be deployed quickly in the event of war on the continent. Chamberlain shot the request down, and for good reasons. The economy was shaky, and the people of Britain were not in favor of involving themselves in war on the continent. But it should also be noted that in 1939, when Hitler invaded Czechoslovakia, he had only twelve divisions holding his western flank. If Britain had seventeen solid divisions available, and the French had been inspired by the British example to provide another ten out of their sixty, the allies might have rolled straight into Berlin and put a stop to Hitler's aggressive tactics then and there. But Chamberlain decided instead that a defensive strategy would deter Hitler.

This left him in a position of trying to threaten a man whom he could defeat only in a protracted war of several years' duration. Britain had no way to project strength into Germany, especially during the German arms build up when Hitler was still weak. The idea that Hitler would be restrained by a power that could not hurt him in the immediate future was one of Chamberlain's worst miscalculations based on his repeated pattern of wishful thinking, especially given that Hitler's expansion would render him almost invulnerable to a blockade. Even after Germany invaded Czechoslovakia, Chamberlain's rearmament efforts were defensive in nature and fell far short of the great effort called for by Eden.

Chamberlain resisted calls to bring Winston Churchill into his cabinet. Churchill had been calling for rearmament for years and had been part of the cabinets that had steered Britain through World War I. He could have offered great insight into the decisions required to prepare for war. But Chamberlain was so confident in his strategy of appeasement that he did not want to risk bringing to power someone who might oppose him.

After Hitler's invasion of Czechoslovakia and takeover of Prague, the next major target was Poland. The immediate point of contention was Danzig, a German-speaking "free city" under the protection of the League of Nations and not yet part of the German state, the Reich that was separated from the rest of the country by a strip of Polish territory. Stung by the humiliating events in Czechoslovakia, Britain joined with France to guarantee Poland's independence against Germany. It was a poor decision. Due to geography and their defensive-based state of armament, Britain and France could not credibly project power into Germany and Poland.

In July 1939 Chamberlain was still optimistic:

> One thing is I think clear, namely that Hitler has concluded that we mean business and that the time is not ripe for the major war. . . . You don't need offensive forces sufficient to win a smashing victory. What you want are defensive forces sufficiently strong to make it impossible for the other side to win except at such cost as to make it not worthwhile.[41]

He was wrong again. Germany remained bellicose. On September 1, 1939, German troops rolled into Poland, England and France were forced to act on their guarantees of Polish freedom, and World War II had begun.

One defense for Chamberlain's policies has been the assertion that Britain's defense capabilities were in such a poor state that military action against Germany was not an option and that the only prudent course was to use appeasement to buy time. There are two arguments against letting this point distract us from the wishful-thinking component of Chamberlain's position.

1. The fact that this state of weakness was allowed to go on for so long argues that it was not something that the prime minister and his government were working hard to change.

2. Evidence exists that Chamberlain was not thinking about delaying war but about preventing it. His friend Horace Wilson stated: "Our

policy was never designed just to postpone war, or enable us to enter war more united. The aim of appeasement was to avoid war altogether, for all time."[42]

Note in Wilson's words the idea that appeasement would prevent war forever; that is, if you give the bully what he wants, he will stop bothering you. Few more wishful statements could have been made.

In this case we see the same features that have appeared before: a strong desire to believe, a belief that one has an "edge," and keeping dissenting voices (like Churchill) as far away as possible.

In another case of appeasement, that of the western powers appeasing Joseph Stalin and the Soviet Union after World War II, President Franklin Roosevelt had a feeling about Stalin similar to Chamberlain's about Hitler. When one of his advisors tried to make clear to him Stalin's perfidiousness, he replied:

> I don't dispute your facts, they are accurate. I don't dispute the logic of your reasoning. I just have a hunch that Stalin is not that kind of man. Harry [Hopkins another advisor] says he's not and that he doesn't want anything but security for his country, and I think that if I give him everything I possibly can and ask nothing from him in return, noblesse oblige, he won't try to annex anything and will work with me for a world of democracy and peace.[43]

We now know, as Roosevelt should have then, that Stalin had no more interest in democracy than a monkey had in square dancing, and probably held a similar view: It was an inexplicable practice of another species but of no concern to him. In comparison with Chamberlain, Roosevelt had few options, and although his appeasement was not truly successful, at least it accomplished more than Chamberlain's. It may even have been the best policy available at the time, but his read on Stalin was dead wrong, just as Chamberlain's read on Hitler was dead wrong. This is yet another example of the wishful thinker's need for an edge.

Medical Quackery

The history of medicine is inextricably intertwined with the history of quackery. This isn't much of a surprise, given that it has only been in the last 100 years or so that real science has brought itself to bear on medicine, and it has produced tremendous results. But legitimate medicine can't cure everything. And when it can't, the door is opened for anyone with a scheme that sounds plausible but only serves to separate the afflicted from their money.

Quackery got off to a running start in the United States in the 1800s, a time when most physicians learned their trade in apprenticeships rather than at medical school, as is the case today. Since you didn't need any formal qualifications at all to practice medicine, quackery was rampant. False advertising for cure-all concoctions was expected, the bolder the better. Eventually the formation of the American Medical Association in 1847 worked against quackery, and the Pure Food and Drug Act of 1906 drove the worst of the charlatans out of business. But today there is still plenty of scope for quackery, especially when perpetrators can set up shop in Mexico and do business essentially untouched by the law.

Bob McCoy, who runs the Museum of Questionable Medical Devices in Minnesota, divides quacks into three groups: the charlatans, who are conscious con artists; the wishful thinkers, who simply don't understand medicine and sincerely believe in their own cures; and the delusional quacks, who have a paranoid worldview and think the medical establishment is out to get them and that only they have the real answer to anything. I believe that the delusional quacks are basically intense versions of the wishful thinkers and that the charlatans also depend on their victims' wishful thinking to ready them for fleecing. Therefore, medical quackery is fundamentally a problem of wishful thinking.

The harm of medical quackery is not in the terminal cases. If normal medical science can offer no hope, there is nothing lost by letting patients try something outside the mainstream. The real harm is in the cases, like those to be discussed, where victims have other options. These may be unpleasant: No one likes the idea of disfiguring surgery, but nevertheless they are options likely to preserve an individual's life.

Most of western medicine is based on evidence. Quackery, however, is generally based on anecdote; this difference is important. Evidence is obtained systematically, it is reviewed by others, it is public and verifiable, and it includes data about when the treatment did not work. Anecdote, however, is gathered haphazardly, is often impossible to verify, is rarely looked at by anyone outside the inner circle of those presenting it, and never mentions the times the treatment didn't work.

Quackery often depends on some underlying theory that sounds plausible but is at best oversimplified; more often it is simply untrue. This is the wishful edge we have seen before. A good example of this is the case of Debbie Benson, who was taking infusions designed to remove pesticides from her body in the belief that this would eliminate her cancer. This is a reasonable-sounding approach, especially if you believe that pesticides are slipping into our food illegally. There is perfectly good scientific evidence that some pesticides are carcinogens, at least in some species. But they are present in our foods in such minute amounts that the likelihood of their being responsible for a particular person's cancer is small, and more important, there is no evidence that removing them will stop a cancer already in progress or that the infusions could remove pesticides that might be lurking in the body.

Below is a heartbreaking case, taken from the excellent "Quackwatch" website, written by a friend of the victim, showing this dynamic: a victim with a strong desire to avoid traditional medical treatment and a group of quacks, some probably well intentioned and some simply out for a fast buck, taking advantage of her.[44]

> My good friend Debbie Benson died July 15, 1997, at age fifty-five. I had known her for thirty years. Her official diagnosis was breast cancer, but she was really a victim of quackery. Conventional treatment might have saved her, but she rejected the advice of her oncologist and went to "natural healers."
>
> Debbie was a registered nurse at the Kaiser hospital in Portland, Oregon, but she had a deep distrust of standard medical practice. She didn't have a mammogram for nine years, and when she did—in March 1996—it showed a cancerous lump in her breast. She had the lump removed, but she refused the additional treatment her doctor recommended. Instead she went to a naturopath who gave her—among other things—some "Pesticide Removal Tinctures."
>
> Soon after that, lymph nodes swelled in Debbie's armpit. The naturopath said that this was merely the effect of the herbal remedies he was giving her and not to worry. Belatedly, she returned to her oncologist at Kaiser hospital, where the lymph nodes were biopsied and found to be cancerous. Once again, she refused the recommended treatment. Unfortunately, the cancer was spreading throughout her body.
>
> Debbie continued to patronize "alternative healers" in the Portland area. One even claimed to diagnose her with a pendulum! She found another

lump in her breast, but the cancer had invaded her liver and was no longer treatable by standard methods.

During the last weeks of her life, another naturopath gave Debbie a skin preparation that was supposed to draw the tumor out of her. This stuff caused an ugly open sore on her breast. By this time, her liver was failing and she felt awful. The naturopath told Debbie she was feeling bad as a result of this medicine, and to get more sleep. When Debbie became too weak to get out of bed and the imminence of her death was obvious, the naturopath blamed Debbie's turn for the worse on "giving up."

I have reported Debbie's mistreatment to state regulatory agencies, and they are investigating.

Debbie and others like her are reasonably intelligent individuals. The terrible thing about this and many similar cases is that they probably did not have to die when they did. Most breast cancers are treatable, especially when detected reasonably early. Unfortunately, people sometimes are unable to believe in the techniques that could save their lives.

What about the people who victimize those like Debbie Benson? I don't believe that many people get up in the morning thinking that today they are going to commit a fraud on another person that will eventually result in that person's death. Thus I can only conclude that these practitioners believed in their own remedies for the most part and that as they watched their patients die, they were unable to break through the barrier of their own wishful thinking, pride, and ignorance, and admit that this situation had gone beyond them.

Missing Airport

We are all familiar with the phenomenon of wishful not-thinking, the practice of refusing to consider the stupidity of something that you know you are going to do anyway. It is linked in my mind to the adolescent feelings of invulnerability that many of us feel lucky to have survived.

That isn't to say that this behavior doesn't crop up all over the place. I first gave it the name of "wishful not-thinking" when a director in a fairly large information systems shop told me this story:

> We needed someone with a very specific expertise in a type of code that isn't used much anymore and is no longer supported by its original

vendor. The code we had to fix needed some immediate changes, and if we didn't get them accomplished there were going to be some fairly harsh consequences. After a whirlwind search we finally found a man who had the background on his resume that we needed. At this point we were within weeks of our deadline. The normal process we went through at that time for a position like this involved a background check to verify things like academic degrees, but we wanted to get this guy started so bad that we had HR skip that part and just bring the man in. It turned out that his resume was falsified and he was betting that he could pick up what he needed on the fly. If we had done our checks, we would have found this out, but we didn't think it was important, as thorough procedures like this aren't necessary when you're doing something vital. As it was, we found out the hard way when he couldn't do the work.

In these cases, you know the right thing to do. You know that you should do the background check, you know that you shouldn't stand on the hood of your friend's car while he careens down back roads in a stumbling drunken stupor with his headlights off, but you don't give the doubt a chance to work in your mind. "It can't happen this time," you think; you act like you are invulnerable. The wish in this case seems to suspend anxiety, which may be a good thing sometimes. However, when something important depends on being anxious enough to keep it in the front of your mind, it's a bad trade.

Cases of ignoring the rules you know you should follow because "it can't happen to me" are a source of many industrial accidents. Reports from the Occupational Safety and Health Administration show time and again that individuals who are injured often ignored basic safety procedures. These cases also occur in demanding sports like SCUBA diving. People are injured or killed while violating the basic safety rules: They dove while ill, were horribly out of shape, didn't have a buddy, or just didn't pay careful attention to conditions with which they were not familiar. Why were they so careless? Because they were sure that nothing bad could happen to them.

I've chosen the discipline of general aviation to provide an example of this phenomenon, not because it is especially prone to these errors—it isn't—but because the cases are well documented and less technically arcane than those from SCUBA diving.

General aviation is the business of flying small planes for fun and profit. It is distinct from commercial aviation, in which huge numbers of passengers are ferried around the world in meticulously maintained planes by professional pilots. Commercial aviation is highly regulated, general aviation is not, and this gives scope to certain types of errors that would never occur in the commercial world.

This case is taken from Robert Cohn's book, *They Called It Pilot Error: True Stories Behind General Aviation Accidents.*[45] It is the case of two pilots, Mark and Lisa. They met at the airport when Lisa began taking flying lessons. Mark was a senior staff officer at the University of Alabama Medical Center, and Lisa was assistant director of patient services. Both were intelligent, professional individuals.

When a conference that they both expected to attend was scheduled for White Sulphur Springs, West Virginia, a bit over 400 miles from where they lived, they decided to fly there together. Their route would take them from Birmingham, Alabama, to Chattanooga, then to Knoxville, then to Bluefield, then to White Sulphur Springs. As is normal practice they selected an alternate airport that they would go to if their first choice for some reason became impossible; if the weather got bad, for instance, they would land at Lewisburg.

The couple spent several days planning their flight. In doing this Mark looked at the distance they would be flying, the rate at which the plane used fuel, the expected wind conditions, and so forth. His initial calculation showed that it would take three hours and thirty minutes to reach White Sulphur Springs and that the Cessna Skyhawk could fly for four hours and ten minutes. The forty-minute cushion was well within the thirty- to forty-minute Federal Aviation Administration (FAA) suggested minimum. In doing this he took data directly from the Skyhawk's operating manual without doing the kind of tests necessary to tell precisely how much fuel the plane held and how the fuel gauge would track its consumption.

The weather that day was poor but acceptable to fly in, even for pilots like Mark and Lisa who were trained only for visual as opposed to instrument flight, and it was expected to improve a bit as a front to the north moved away.

During the flight the couple took a quick detour to see Lookout Mountain from the air and briefly got lost trying to find their way back to their normal flight path. They had an anxious moment or two but soon found their way and discovered that the wind was pushing them along a bit faster than expected. When the plane passed Bluefield—their last chance to stop for fuel before their destination—the couple thought they still had a cushion of twenty to twenty-five minutes of fuel; in fact, however, their cushion was down to about ten minutes. At this point two factors were working against them: Mark's imprecise calculation of their fuel capacity and the extra gas they burned in their detour. Now a third factor came into play: the weather.

As the plane neared Lewisburg (they had chosen to land at a larger airport there rather than at White Sulphur Springs), the wind picked up, giving them a little more boost, but neither noticed it. The bad weather that had been to their north moved directly down on them and the Lewisburg airport shut down for Visual Flight Rules, for pilots not trained in Instrument Flight Rules, or IFR. The following exchange took place between Mark and the Lewisburg tower:

Lewisburg: Say your Position, this is Lewisburg.

Mark: 18 to 20 miles southwest at 3,100 feet, landing Lewisburg.

Lewisburg: Lewisburg went IFR [instrument flight rules] about ten minutes ago. We're now 800 and 2 1/2 in light to moderate rain. We don't expect any improvement for at least an hour. Suggest you try Roanoake or Bluefield. The weather system that's affecting us has been moving in from the North.

Mark: Uh, Lewisburg, any chance for a special VFR, sir. We're low on fuel.

Lewisburg: Sorry, this is mountain country, sir, and our conditions are getting worse, not better. Suggest you head for an alternate immediately.

Mark: Lewisburg, we're very low on fuel. We really need that special VFR.

Lewisburg: The way this weather's coming in, we might be below IFR minimums by the time you get here. Roanoke's weather is fine and you'll have a tailwind getting there. That's your best choice, sir.

Mark and Lisa chose instead to head back to Bluefield, which they were sure they could find. The strong tailwind that had been helping them was now blowing them backward, and they inched forward into its teeth. About eighteen miles from the airport, the engine quit. Mark did a good job of landing in a rocky field, but the plane dove forward on its nose. Mark and Lisa were battered, but alive and ready to think about what went wrong. Mark had this to say about the accident:

> Oh, we started out mad at Cessna for not making it clear that EMPTY meant EMPTY for real. And we complained to the FAA that the FARs (Federal Aviation Regulations) in general and the fuel reserve requirements in particular were written by people who have no understanding of

who reads them and how the regs might be misinterpreted. But that was all grousing. We know how to read. We know how to count. We're both pilots and we should have used our heads and landed at Mercer County [the airport at Bluefield].

An FAA representative had this to say about the accident:

> Every time there's a fuel exhaustion accident—which by the way, is the cause of one out of every 12 general aviation fatalities—we hear the same stories: "The airplane had a higher fuel consumption rate than it ever had before. The engine quit the very second the needle in the fuel gauge read EMPTY. We planned our ground speed conservatively. Our navigating was close to perfect and couldn't have been off by more than 10 minutes or so. The weather changed on us very suddenly."
>
> There might be a couple more I've forgotten, but to every story I say "baloney," and I'm not trying to be a wise guy or a Monday morning quarterback. Whenever we do some further checking into one of these cases we invariably find wishful thinking, carelessness, negligence, and rationalization, which in my book is all baloney.

This was the problem; our wishful-thinking wiring can suppress the anxiety that makes us think about what might be necessary. The signs were there for Mark and Lisa (who were eventually married, by the way). They knew they were low on fuel, they knew there was inclement weather in the area, but they wished away the seriousness of it, and they're lucky to be alive.

▪ NOTES

1. Rebecca Henry, "The Effects of Choice and Incentives on the Overestimation of Future Performance," *Organizational Behavior and Human Decision Processes* 57 (1994): 210–225.
2. N. D. Weinstein, "Unrealistic Optimism about Future Life Events," *Journal of Personality and Social Psychology* 39 (1980): 806–820.
3. M. Seligman, *Learned Optimism* (New York: Alfred A. Knopf, 1990).
4. Harry Houdini, *A Magician Among the Spirits* (New York: Harper & Row, 1926).
5. Joe Nickell, "Undercover Among the Spirits. Investigating Camp Chesterfield," *Skeptical Inquirer* 26, No. 2 (March/April 2002).
6. M. Lamar Keene, *The Psychic Mafia* (New York: Prometheus Books, 1997).
7. Daniel Stashower, *Teller of Tales: The Life of Arthur Conan Doyle* (New York: Henry Holt and Co., 1999).

8. Arthur Conan Doyle, *The New Revelation* (London: Hodder & Stoughton, 1918).

9. Arthur Conan Doyle, *The New Revelation* (London: Hodder & Stoughton, 1918).

10. Arthur Conan Doyle, *The Stark Munro Letters* (London: Longmans, Green and Co., 1895).

11. Daniel Stashower, *Teller of Tales: The Life of Arthur Conan Doyle* (New York: Henry Holt and Co., 1999).

12. Daniel Stashower, *Teller of Tales: The Life of Arthur Conan Doyle* (New York: Henry Holt and Co., 1999).

13. Massimo Polidoro, *Final Séance: The Strange Friendship Between Houdini and Conan Doyle* (New York: Prometheus Books, 2001).

14. Arthur Conan Doyle, *The History of Spiritualism* (London: Constable, 1926).

15. Massimo Polidoro, *Final Séance: The Strange Friendship Between Houdini and Conan Doyle* (New York: Prometheus Books, 2001).

16. Daniel Stashower, *Teller of Tales: The Life of Arthur Conan Doyle* (New York: Henry Holt and Co., 1999).

17. Massimo Polidoro, *Final Séance: The Strange Friendship Between Houdini and Conan Doyle* (New York: Prometheus Books, 2001).

18. Ibid.

19. Conan Doyle, *The Coming of the Fairies* (London: Hodder & Stoughton, 1921).

20. John Kenneth Galbraith, *A Short History of Financial Euphoria* (New York: Penguin Books, 1990).

21. Edward Chancellor, *Devil Take the Hindmost* (New York: Farrar, Straus and Giroux, 1999).

22. John Kenneth Galbraith, *A Short History of Financial Euphoria* (New York: Penguin Books, 1990).

23. Ibid.

24. J. Kaplan Philip, *F'd Companies: Spectacular Dot-com Flameouts* (New York: Simon & Schuster, 2002).

25. John A. Byrne, "The Fall of a Dot-Com," *Business Week,* May 1, 2000.

26. Ibid.

27. John Cassidy, *Dot.com: The Greatest Story Ever Sold* (New York: HarperCollins, 2002).

28. John A. Byrne, "The Fall of a Dot-Com," *Business Week,* May 1, 2000.

29. Chris Nerney, "Second Act Doubtful for Valueless America," August 14, 2000, www.internetstockreport.com.

30. *Webster's New Universal Unabridged Dictionary* (New York: Simon & Schuster, 1983).

31. Sydney Astor, "Guilty Men: The Case of Neville Chamberlain," *The Origins of the Second World War,* ed. Patrick Finney (London: Arnold, 1997).

32. Stephen Rock, *Appeasement in International Politics* (Lexington: University Press of Kentucky, 2000).

33. R. A. C. Parker, *Chamberlain and Appeasement: British Policy and the Coming of the Second World War* (New York: St. Martin's Press, 1993).

34. Ibid.

35. Ibid.

36. Ibid.
37. Donald Watt, *How War Came: The Immediate Origins of the Second World War 1938– 1939* (New York: Pantheon Books, 1989).
38. Sydney Astor, "Guilty Men: The Case of Neville Chamberlain," *The Origins of the Second World War*, ed. Patrick Finney (London: Arnold, 1997).
39. Ibid.
40. Ibid.
41. Ibid.
42. R. A. C. Parker, *Chamberlain and Appeasement: British Policy and the Coming of the Second World War* (New York: St. Martin's Press, 1993).
43. Ibid.
44. Kenneth Spiker, "The Death of Debbie Benson," www.quackwatch.com/ 01quackeryRelatedtopics/victims/debbie.html.
45. Robert L. Cohn, *They Called It Pilot Error: True Stories Behind General Aviation Accidents* (New York: Tab Books, 1994).

Mythical Thinking

e all have beliefs. Perhaps, for instance, I have a belief system that describes disease as something caused by evil spirits invading the body. Given that, I might decide that the way to cure a disease is to put on a spooky mask and dance around the patient to scare away the spirits. It won't work often, but sometimes people will get better anyway, and pretty soon nothing short of a traumatic failure of this theory is going to change my mind. I will be stuck in this myth I have created about the way the world works.

The above illustrates the essence of mythical thinking. It occurs when our thought patterns are so colored by our view of the world that when that view is proved false, or when it does not apply, we are unable to adjust. The story, or "myth," has taken such control of our thought process that we are unable to see an alternative. Mythical thinking is about not being able to change your mind.

A belief system or knowledge structure like this has sometimes been called a "schema" (plural schemata). It is a model of the world that describes a certain situation and tells us how to look at things. It is a theory of how things work, a mind-set.

These schemas are wonderful and necessary. The time and energy humans have to spend thinking about things is limited. We have to have sets of assumptions about the way the world works or we'd never come to a decision on anything. When your alarm clock goes off in the morning, you do not stop to think that the noise you hear might be coming from a man with a bell who has infiltrated your house and is intent on waking you up early. You don't worry that you might have been drugged in your sleep and placed in a room designed to look just like your bedroom, with a person who looks just like your spouse in bed next to you. You have to make a few assumptions. This is the logical thing to do; it's unlikely that someone could get into your house without your taking notice, nobody snores just like your spouse, and so forth. We couldn't live without this kind of structure.

The vast majority of these structures serve us pretty well, but what happens when one of our "how the world works" stories is wrong? We might call an incorrect schema a "myth." It's something that brings order to our thoughts but doesn't actually reflect reality. It's like the way ancient peoples might have attributed thunder to a large-muscled god having a game of tenpins rather than the expansion of air superheated by lightning. We will see that the followers of Mrs. Marian Keech had myths about the end of the world, British admirals had myths about the supremacy of the wooden sailing ship, and British generals had myths about the value of cavalry, especially in comparison to the tank.

The most interesting thing about our myths is that we are remarkably resistant to changing them. Changing a bedrock belief has all kinds of painful effects. For one thing, there is the sheer anxiety produced by admitting to ourselves that we don't actually know how the world works after all. Think about the last time you were in a situation that you had absolutely no preparation for. For me, for instance, it is very stressful to attempt any type of home repair. I have little knowledge of these operations and always suspect that whatever pipe, wire, or beam I am fiddling with is a crucial component that will flood, burn, or collapse the house if not handled just so. I always imagine a skilled workman looking up from picking through the ruins of the house, an amazed expression on his face, saying: "Oh jeez, you messed with THAT?" It is stressful to admit ignorance, so I call someone with the skills to do the job.

Another reason our basic worldviews are hard to change is that we may have some ego tied up with them. For instance, if you believe that your nation is basically moral and just, it will be unpleasant to be told that some of your countrymen are engaged in systematic atrocity. This is one reason that many Germans had trouble believing in the extent of the Holocaust. In this way mythical and wishful thinking are often found together.

Like the other error types discussed in this book, mythical thinking has some common characteristics:

- **Commitment.** When a person makes a commitment to a "way of thought," especially if it is public or painful, such as with the Keech prophesies, it is very difficult for him or her to escape the myth.

- **Group support and elimination of the nonbeliever.** When a person is surrounded by believers, group pressures make it more difficult to escape the myth. The group can provide an element of tribal thinking, as we shall see in Chapter 4. In order to retain the myth, the group will act to silence opinions contrary to its belief and avoid those who do not share the myth. Cults with weird beliefs typically shut themselves away from the world to avoid the need to hear nonconforming beliefs, for instance.

- **Personal benefit or comfort.** When the myth is one that casts the person in a good light, thus providing ego gratification, or when it provides other benefits, such as keeping the person's skill valuable and maintaining prestige, as in the case of cavalry opposition to tanks, the myth is more difficult to escape. This adds the power of wishful thinking to the myth. Some myths are "comfort" beliefs: They make it possible for us to go through life without worrying about death, for instance, because we know it isn't the end.

- **Previous success.** When the myth is associated with success, especially long-term dominance, as in the case of the British military, it is difficult to escape. In this way wishful thinking and mythical thinking are linked and thus are often found together.

- **Rationalization.** Myths are sometimes called "self-sealing belief systems." If you challenge people who have an absurd worldview on some subject, their rationalizations become more and more ridiculous. We will see this several times in the cases to be discussed as believers struggle to retain their myths.

- **Lack of objective data.** The only way to explode a dearly held myth is with painful real world experience. Situations that make this experience difficult to obtain, such as a prolonged dominance in the commercial world or a long period of peace for a military, make it difficult to escape from a mythical thought pattern. Lack of good information allows the thinker to focus only on data that supports the myth.

SCIENCE

Mythical thinking is especially important to the topic of smart people doing dumb things. David Perkins, a professor in the Graduate School of

Education at Harvard, has done some interesting research on the way people see only one side of an argument and how hard we work to keep from changing our minds about our beliefs. Perkins reports on his research in his book *Outsmarting IQ*.[1] Perkins and his team interviewed over 300 people about issues of the day, such as the desirability of a freeze on nuclear weapons development and a local bottle law that would require a deposit on beverage containers. They looked at the arguments people put forward not with an eye to which were right or wrong but to understanding the reasoning used. Their findings are fascinating.

First, Perkins and company found that most people do not understand, or at least do not act on, the idea that you must understand both sides of a question before you can give an informed opinion. Typically the subjects were not able to give a reason to support the side of the issue they did not agree with. In addition, they didn't seem to explore the weaknesses in their own arguments. For instance, if people believed that fewer nuclear weapons was good, they did not seem to think about the fact (or at least the plausible counterargument) that any number of weapons greater than zero can start a war.

Second, Perkins and his associates found that people are quite capable of seeing the other side if they are pointed in that direction. When directly asked for counterarguments, people were able to develop them, but most people seemed to find a few arguments for one side, then stopped thinking.

Third, and most interesting to us regarding the mistakes made by smart people, Perkins and his team found that the ability to avoid "my side" bias was not impacted by age or level of education, but it did correlate with intelligence (as measured by an IQ test), though not in the way you would expect. Intelligent people tended to produce more complex and elaborate defenses for their own side of an argument but to be no more likely to look at the other side. The natural consequence of this is that it will be even harder for more intelligent people to abandon a wrongheaded idea since they are better at coming up with reasons to justify it.

Another key concept in talking about our unwillingness to change a mind-set is the idea of making a commitment and the impact that has on our thoughts. We want to be consistent. Once we take an action, doing something inconsistent with that action is difficult for us. Being consistent is considered a sign of intelligence and of having a well-balanced personality.

In one experiment researchers had the subjects estimate the length of a line. One group of subjects simply noted mentally what their estimate was; another wrote their estimates down on an erasable pad (the kind with a plastic cover that you lift to erase everything on the pad); and a third group wrote their estimates publicly and signed their name to them. All subjects were then shown evidence that their estimates were incorrect.

The group that had not recorded their findings showed the least resistance to the new data and were fairly willing to change their estimates. The group that had written and erased their guesses showed more resistance, and the group that had publicly noted their original estimates was the least likely to change their estimates of the length of the lines. In the third case tribal thinking, something we will look at in Chapter 4, was probably kicking in to make people worry about how they appeared to the rest of the group. But the second case, where all the subjects had done was write down and erase their estimate, clearly shows consistency bias. A small myth had formed in people's minds simply because they had actively made a commitment by writing down their estimate.

Because religious belief generally involves visible public commitment, some of the most interesting examples of this type of mistake come from the world of religion. Everyone knows the story of how Galileo was persecuted by the church, even though anyone could have looked through a telescope and seen the evidence proving that Earth was not the center of the universe. Religious groups also resisted evolution when it was first proposed, and some continue to resist it today. Thus, we look first at a pseudoreligious example of the power to retain a mind-set.

Cases

Failures of Prophecy: The Myth of the End of the World

As long as anyone can remember, humanity has amused itself by predicting the future. We have sought to divine the shape of things to come by looking at Tarot cards, the leaves left after a cup of tea has been drunk, the lines on a person's palm, the entrails of slaughtered animals, the stars on the night of one's birth, the migratory patterns of various fowl, and the way a bone cracks when we throw it in the fire.

For various reasons these things sometimes seem to work, and when they don't there are plenty of excuses: The spirits were angry, whatever.

For our purposes here, though, we have a more interesting aspect of prophecy to consider. What happens to people's beliefs when a specific and verifiable prophecy comes up completely wrong?

One of the most interesting and well-documented examples of this concerns Mrs. Marian Keech and a small band of followers in Ohio in the mid-1950s who believed that the world was about to end and were kind enough to provide a date for the event. This instance is so well understood because the group was infiltrated by a hardy band of sociologists well before the date in question. These investigators were then able to observe the actions of the group members leading up to the date, during that time period, and after the predicted cataclysm failed to occur. The discussion that follows is based on information in a book by the sociologists who investigated the group, L. Festinger, H. W. Riecken, and S. Schacter, *When Prophecy Fails.*[2]

The story centers on Marian Keech, a longtime student of the occult. About the time these events begin Mrs. Keech, who had become interested in flying saucers, made an interesting discovery.

> I had a feeling that someone was trying to get my attention. Without knowing why, I picked up a pencil and a pad that were lying on the table near my bed. My hand began to write in another handwriting. I realized that somebody else was using my hand, and I said: "Will you identify yourself?" And they did. I was much surprised to find that it was my father, who had passed away.

Automatic writing is a well-known phenomenon in the occult world and is frequently used to "channel" spirits. The process seems to function, at least sometimes, without the conscious awareness of the writer. The writer isn't "crazy," as such, although some practitioners come up with such bizarre statements that one could question their link to reality. Mrs. Keech was probably familiar with automatic writing, given her background in mysticism.

With time Mrs. Keech became able to receive messages from spirits other than her father. These beings were generally spiritually advanced and treated her as a student. She eventually settled with a mentor named Sananda from the planet Clarion. Sananda let Mrs. Keech know that he was the modern-day incarnation of the Bible's Jesus.

It is worth pointing out at this point that Mrs. Keech and her followers were not "crazy," and neither were they stupid, as bizarre as their belief system was. While their beliefs were outside the mainstream, many people hold similar beliefs, even if they do not extend quite as far. Many of Mrs. Keech's followers were educated and among her fifteen to twenty fairly regular students, there were a medical doctor and a PhD technical researcher, as well as a number of college students who, if naive, at least had a degree of native intellectual ability.

Mrs. Keech received regular messages from Sananda describing the universe, its inhabitants, and the place of Mrs. Keech's group in it. The picture that emerges—that of angelic aliens who want to help us but choose to do so by sending telepathic messages to a midwestern housewife—seems strange to most of us, but its individual elements are not unusual in the history of religious belief. Sananda describes his planet of Clarion as a perfect place with no death or want, something of a "heaven." He promises to watch over the Keech group and assures them that Earth's evildoers will be punished.

These ideas are common to many religions, although in this case they are mixed up in a strange way with talk of flying saucers. Sananda is very nonthreatening, his message is optimistic, and he wants to help us advance.

There is more to Mrs. Keech's teaching than can be covered briefly. In her Sananda-inspired writings, however, she was told many times that she and her people would be protected and was continually exhorted to have faith and patience. There were many simple instructions to "seek the light." Her world was divided into forces of light and those of darkness. On the side of light were people like herself, her students, and her instructors. Wearing the black hats were warmongers, scientists, and nonbelievers.

Eventually the idea that the world was coming to an end began to creep into Mrs. Keech's writings, first in hints, but eventually she was told that there would be a great wave that would come as far inland as the Rocky Mountains and:

> Yet the land will be as yet not submerged, but as a washing of the top to the sea for the purpose of purifying it of the earthling and the creating the new order. Yet will it be of the LIGHT, for all things must first be likened unto the housecleaning, in which the chaos reigns first, second the ORDER.

THIS IS DATED NOT IN SYMBOLOGY . . . THE REAL!—
REALITY YET.

This was to be a complete remaking of the world; England, France, and Russia would be drowned, while the Egyptian desert would become fertile. Mu (an Atlantis-like continent under the Pacific Ocean) would rise again. Eventually the spirits came across with a date. The cataclysm would occur on December 21, 1955, and all those who were ready—those who were "followers of the light"—would be taken up ahead of time in spaceships. At some point it must have struck Mrs. Keech that wiping out 4 billion people was hardly the act of a group of angelic beings, and it came out in her writings that those who were killed would be reincarnated on planets appropriate to their level of spiritual development.

The final few days before the cataclysm and the period immediately thereafter are a fascinating study for those interested in the capacity of the human mind to hang on to an idea.

By December 17 the group had prepared to be evacuated from the doomed Earth at a moment's notice. They had been instructed by Sananda through Mrs. Keech to remove all metal from their persons. They spent some time ripping the zippers out of pants, taking the clasps off of brassieres, and removing nails from their shoes. Eyeglasses and any form of identification were also forbidden and were likewise put aside. On the morning of December 17 Mrs. Keech received a phone call from a man who identified himself as Captain Video from outer space. He informed the group that a flying saucer would land in Mrs. Keech's backyard to pick them up at 4:00 PM that day. At this point at least one group member suspected a practical joke. She was overruled, however, since it was known that the spacemen could communicate by phone, although sometimes they were forced to use codes when contacting the group in this way.

At 4:00 the faithful were gathered in the Keech kitchen, with metal obediently removed from their persons and their coats in their hands. They waited until 5:30 before giving up. Mrs. Keech refused to discuss the reasons for the saucer's nonappearance, but she soon received another message from Sananda telling her that after the pickup, she would return to "the Father's house" rather than being sent back to Earth. While this temporarily buoyed the group, they eventually fell to discussing why the spacemen had not come. First they turned on the *Captain Video* television show and watched it looking for clues. When that was unsatisfactory, they finally fell to discussing the nonevent themselves. Some felt that the presence of strangers (there were a number of observers and general hangers-on around the Keech house that afternoon) was the problem, but eventually it was determined that this had been in the nature of a drill, a dry run to help them get ready for the real thing.

The group lost a single member at this point: a young girl new to the Keech philosophy left for a Coke with her boyfriend and never came back. The rest of the group remained true.

At about midnight Mrs. Keech received another message from Sananda telling her that the spaceship was on the way at that moment and would not wait if the group members were not ready. The group waited in the cold midwestern December night in Mrs. Keech's backyard, some exercising to get warm. At 1:00 ~AM Mrs. Keech went inside and returned to say that they should continue to wait. At 2:00, with much of the group sitting in a car with the motor running for warmth, Mrs. Keech received another message. This one was a mixture of blessings for those who were patient combined with directions to go back in the house and wait to be contacted by a man who would take them to the pickup site.

This second disappointment left the group subdued but did not break their faith. They had no good explanation for the night's failure and so considered it too "just a drill" and avoided talking about it. During the day on the eighteenth Mrs. Keech received another message, with one point she considered worth emphasizing. Sananda said through her: "I have never been tardy; I have never kept you waiting; I have never disappointed you in anything."

The outright falsehood of this message did not strike any of the group. They took it as encouragement.

At about 10:00 ~PM on December 20 the message that set the stage for the penultimate act in the drama arrived from Sananda:

> At the hour of midnight you shall be put into parked cars and taken to a place where ye shall be put aboard a porch [a flying saucer] and ye shall be purposed by the time you are there. . . . and at no time are you to ask what is what and not a plan shall go astray.

The final ten minutes of waiting were tense. The group sat with their coats in their laps, waiting for salvation. When 12:00 came and went the group did nothing. Finally Mrs. Keech got a message from Sananda telling the group to break for coffee. During this break Mrs. Keech made the following statement:

> Well, all right. Suppose they gave us a wrong date. Well, this only got into the newspapers on Thursday and people had only 72 hours to get ready to meet their maker. Now suppose it doesn't happen tonight. Let's suppose it happens next year or two years or three or four years from now. I'm not going to change one bit. I'm going to sit here and write and maybe people will say it was this little group spreading light here that prevented the flood. . . . I'm not sorry a bit. I won't be sorry no matter what happens.

The group tried to find an interpretation of the message that would meet with the observed facts. They noted that since parked cars don't move, perhaps this was a metaphor for their own bodies, which were indeed right there at midnight. The porch might then be a symbol for inner knowledge.

One member made this statement to one of the sociologists: "I've had to go a long way. I've given up just about everything. I've cut every tie: I've burned every bridge. I've turned my back on the world. I can't afford to doubt. I have to believe."

This statement shows the role of commitment and consistency in mythical thinking. This group member had become so committed that he was incapable of changing his mind. Finally Mrs. Keech received another message from Sananda:

> mighty is the word of God—and by his word have ye been saved—for from the mouth of death have ye been delivered and at no time has there been such a force loosed upon the Earth. Not since the beginning of time upon this Earth has there been such a force of Good and light as now floods this room and that which had been loosed within this room now floods the entire Earth.

In this way again, a defeat was turned into victory. The promised cataclysm had not arrived because Mrs. Keech's little group had flooded the world with so much light that it no longer needed to be saved. While most unbiased observers would call this a convenient way to get out of a failed prediction, at least some of the group accepted it.

A few group members, along with Mrs. Keech, did not lose faith in their myth after the final failure; one actually went on the road to talk to other groups about flying saucers and his revelations. But what about the other group members? We might expect that those who were not quite as close to the inner circle might leave, and some did. But some did not.

In general, those who were not present to get immediate support from other members of the group lost faith to a greater degree than those who were with the group.

Another member was disillusioned, although not completely. He still thought that Mrs. Keech was receiving genuine messages, although she was getting some of them wrong. But at the same time the incident prompted him to give a bit of critical thought to the whole situation: "When you stop and think of it, it seems rather cruel to drown all these people just to teach them a lesson, doesn't it?"

This is actually typical of people who have had their beliefs challenged: They find the smallest possible piece of the myth to give up.

The Keech group broke up soon after the final debacle. Mrs. Keech's habit of expounding on her beliefs to the local grade school children had finally gotten under local parents' skin, which made the area inhospitable for her. She moved away, but she kept in touch with the faithful by mail thereafter.

In reading the Keech case, it is difficult not to dismiss the group as idiots or as least unduly credulous. The phone call from "Captain Video" should have sent any reasonable person screaming from the room. Unfortunately, the behavior of the group is not unusual in cases of failed prophecy. It is fairly common for group members to employ absurd rationalizations in cases like this. They may contend, as the Keech group did, that they have prevented the end of the world, or that the prophecy was just a test, or that the end of the world happened but was on another plane of existence where humans wouldn't notice (I'm not making that up). It is interesting to note that while some of Mrs. Keech's followers lost faith in her, only a minority lost faith in the ideas that space aliens might really be communicating with Earth by psychic means, that these same angelic beings were thinking about destroying the planet, and that you could "spread light" enough to save the planet without leaving the house.

It is also worth noting that Mrs. Keech was not a charismatic woman. It was the myth she put forth, not the force of her personality, that kept her group together, and some of them held to parts of the myth even when they fell away from her group.

Whereas some people read the Keech case as a comedy about a group of hopelessly self-absorbed, privileged nincompoops, others see a desperate band of people trying to find meaning in their lives. What we can't do is dismiss them as so unlike ourselves that we could never make those mistakes; we all do, just on a more reasonable scale.

Although not stupid in a conventional sense, Mrs. Keech and her band of followers were clearly far outside the mainstream. The rest of the cases in this chapter illustrate mythical thinking in more common areas.

Tanks and Horses: The Myth of the Cavalry

I am going to pick on the British military a bit here. This is not because I have anything against the British; I like them. But the British had the misfortune to be the world's dominant military power as the Industrial Revolution changed the face of the planet. Because of this, and because British military leaders were willing to write down what went wrong, they became a great example of how people and groups get stuck in old beliefs. Much of the following discussion is taken from David Divine's book *The Blunted Sword* and Norman Dixon's *On the Psychology of Military Incompetence*.[3]

The 1800s were the century of the Pax Britannia. The British Empire stretched from the East Indies to the West Indies; it included a large part of North America and holdings in Africa, the Middle East, and Asia. The British army stopped Napoleon at Waterloo, and the British navy almost single-handedly put a stop to the slave trade in the Atlantic. The empire was not just superior to any single foe; it was more powerful than most credible combinations of opponents, especially at sea.

Unfortunately, the British Admiralty had a difficult relationship with innovation. British author and defense commentator David Divine has calculated that "of twenty major technological developments from the first marine engine to the Polaris submarine the Admiralty machine has discouraged, delayed, obstructed, or positively rejected seventeen."[4]

The army was little better. In this case we will look at one of the many innovations that the British military machine was unable to grasp due to a conservative mind-set and the inability to see past current practice. We will see that these decision makers were captured by their own myths in a way that seems to be unique to bureaucratic organizations.

The proudest military tradition has always been that of the cavalry. At its very beginning in the West, the cavalry was made up of people who had enough money to afford a horse. They sat up higher than everyone else on the battlefield and ran mere footmen through with long spears without getting blood on their armor. Great commanders from Alexander the Great to George Patton often were cavalrymen.

Horses were beloved by the military men of the 1800s, or perhaps we should say that riding was beloved, since horses themselves come in for much abuse in war. At the very least horses are more lovable than tanks; they are warm to sleep with and you can eat them if you have to. And when there is no war going on, you can ride them around to visit your holdings, or perhaps indulge in a bit of fox hunting or pig sticking.

Unfortunately, horses are not armored, and with the advent of modern weapons, the tank was clearly a better bet for warfare. But officers who had been raised in the cavalry myth wanted nothing to do with the tank and viewed it disparagingly.

The British War Office resisted the introduction of the tank, even after it had been used successfully in World War I; it was not really developed until World War II. Armored warfare was seen as a threat to the supremacy of the cavalry, the glory arm of the army. This perception was off the mark since the machine gun and quick firing rifle had already spelled death for the cavalry as a force in major battles. One observer, Norman Dixon, said this about the slow adoption of armored vehicles:

> It might be concluded . . . (that this) invention was put aside not just because it was a new idea, which it was not, nor because it was not needed, which it was, but because it conflicted with a mystical belief in the virtues of Horsed cavalry and in the power of a prolonged artillery barrage.[5]

By 1914 the British army owned 18 mechanical transport vehicles and 25,000 horses, with another 25,000 in subsidized reserve. Remember, this was at a time when the motorcar was being used regularly in the civilian world. In 1901 A. G. Hales, the correspondent of *The Times* in South Africa, wrote, after watching 448,000 British soldiers trying to defeat 87,000 Boers in the Boer War:

> The Bayonet charge of a few years back is as dead as the Grecian phalanx—the quick firing rifle has changed the face of war. . . . for nineteen dreary months the great English people has been held in check by a handful of farmers, simply because English folk cling to old traditions as sand crabs cling to seaweed. . . . I used to sit in the saddle and watch the

British attacking a position, and to me it was simply incomprehensible that they did not attempt to evolve a new process of attack which would nullify the natural advantages and native astuteness of the Boers. . . . If the British . . . had constructed armored motor cars they could at once have nullified the advantages the Boers possessed . . . but England seems strangely apathetic on the subject.[6]

The next chapter of this tale is very interesting and subtle. Lieutenant-Colonel E. D. Swinton, a historian and expert on the use of machine guns, began thinking about how troops could cross broken terrain in the face of machine gun fire. After hearing from a mining engineer about the capabilities of the American Holt tractor, he tried to interest the British War Office in the idea of a treaded vehicle to overcome enemy trenches. There was no interest. However, the idea made its way to Winston Churchill, then First Lord of the Admiralty, who was already interested in the idea of tractor vehicles. Whatever other talents and flaws Churchill possessed he was, at least in this case, a military visionary. For a while tank development went forward under the direction not of the army but of the navy, where they were called "landships." Eventually, in 1916, the tank was demonstrated to a group of senior officers and performed admirably, showing its ability to cross trenches as wide as nine feet. Despite this Lord Kitchner, then in the War Office, commented that the tank was a "pretty mechanical toy . . . the war will never be won by such machines."[7]

Britain was desperate, however. Field Marshal Douglas Haig, who commanded the army, was frantic for anything that might end the deadly stalemate of trench warfare of World War I and provide an alternative to massed frontal assault on enemy trenches where victory could be measured by yards gained per 1,000 men lost. Haig was also known to have been wrong about the machine gun, calling it a "much overrated weapon," and may have decided to be more open to accepting new technology. Against the advice of the army's tank experts, he rushed the small number of machines he could obtain into combat before they were ready and before there were enough of them to make a difference. The attack was a failure, many of the vehicles failed to start and those that did were knocked out by enemy fire.

After this first debacle, the opponents of the tank leapt to the attack. They focused on minor failings of the new approach and leveled insignificant criticisms, focusing on them to the exclusion of everything else. This is a common response when one's myth is threatened; we saw it in the selective hearing of the Keech group. Focusing on confirming evidence and ignoring disconfirming evidence is a powerful cause of error.

Later, in November of 1917, the British used tanks successfully at Cambrai in France. It is useful to look at this battle since it shows the position of both tanks and cavalry in what was to be the new world of war, and it clarifies the attitude of the commanders.

General George Harper commanded a section in the center of the British line and was supposed to follow the tank penetration of the enemy lines and capture a key village, Flesquieres. He was of the old school, an infantry commander who had no use for armored vehicles. Harper's performance was a classic in the annals of passive resistance. He never refused to work with the tanks or did anything that could be construed as not going along with the program, but nevertheless he avoided doing anything at all to help the new technology succeed.

Initially the 1917 tank offensive at Cambrai was a spectacular success. The tanks overran three lines of strongly fortified German trenches and gained over four miles across a six-mile front. This was an unheard-of success at that point in the war.

Upon seeing this initial success, a good general would have committed his forces to keep them connected with the tanks that spearheaded the offensive. Harper chose instead to wait to send his troops forward until the scheduled time, thus leaving the tanks without infantry support. In all he delayed about an hour. This gave the Germans time to bring up field guns to command the area through which the tanks had to pass. Bryan Cooper, in his book *The Ironclads of Cambrai,* gives this description:

> Had the infantry been close behind the tanks as Fuller (the tactician who had designed the British approach) had planned, they could easily have dealt with these guns in a matter of minutes, but the infantry were far behind. With such perfect targets the German gunners opened fire. One by one the tanks were hit, while the crews worked desperately at the cumbersome gears to drive a zig-zag course and the gunners tried to return the fire.[8]

Harper's deliberate slowdown in the center of the battle had brought the tank penetration there to a halt and destroyed many of the new machines.

Next, the cavalry was supposed to move forward and exploit the breach created by the tanks. Harper's delay cost the attack some time and allowed the

Germans to regroup. The battle of Cambrai came to an end with the allies gaining a significant piece of ground, but not breaking open the German lines as intended.

Cambrai should have been an illuminating experience. Actually it should have happened sooner. Winston Churchill, one of the early proponents of the tank, was later to write in his book *The World Crisis*:

> Accusing as I do without exception all the great Allied offensives of 1914, 1916, and 1917, as needless and wrongly conceived operations of infinite cost, I am bound to reply to the question—what else could be done? And I answer it, pointing to the Battle of Cambrai, "this could have been done." This in many variants, this in larger and better forms ought to have been done, and would have been done if only the generals had not been content to fight machine-gun bullets with the breasts of gallant men and think that that was waging war.[9]

In a triumph of mythical thinking, the cavalrymen found a single item to focus on and excluded everything else from their thoughts. They fixated on a successful use of cavalry in a flanking movement against the Turkish army in Palestine in which a few tanks had been unable to pursue the Turks. The cavalrymen took this to mean that the horse would forever be able to outmaneuver the tank.

Nothing could have been further from the truth. Smaller tanks would have been able to manage the pursuit easily, and a small number of armored cars actually did precede the cavalry in that chase. A similar event occurred when a rumor surfaced that the Germans had invented a tank-killing superbullet, the "Hagler-Ultra." The cavalrymen were so caught up in the belief (which actually turned out to be propaganda) that the new bullet could stop a tank that no one paused to consider what it might do to a horse.

Once World War I was over, the military attempted to "get back to some real soldiering," in the words of one unidentified warrior. Without an immediate need for armored vehicles, many in power had no use for them. In 1919, two years after success at Cambrai and a year after Amiens, Major-General Sir Louis Jackson said this in a lecture: "The Tank proper was a freak. The circumstances which called it into existence were exceptional and are not likely to recur. If they do, they can be dealt with by other means."[10]

In 1922 an essay competition was held that focused on the organization of the British forces for the next war. One entry was written by Captain Basil Liddell Hart and was titled "Mechanization of the Army." Hart was to become a revered military thinker and in some ways a father of the tactics of mechanized warfare. His essay was not selected; instead a very senior and orthodox panel chose one titled "The Limitations of the Tank." There were allegations that the prize committee had been stacked with old, conservative officers to keep any tank-related nonsense out of the limelight. Hart's essay was published in *Army Quarterly*, where it was read, translated, and disseminated into the German army. It became required reading for the German General Staff and was studied extensively by Heinz Guderian, who came to be known as "Quick Heinz" for his commitment to mechanized warfare. Guderian led the German armor in the initial Blitzkrieg assault on France at the beginning of World War II with spectacular success. By this time Hart had been forced out of the British army.

Hart also wrote a book *Paris, or the Future of War,* which laid out his thoughts about armored tactics.[11] In 1925 Field Marshal Haig, the man who had created such a dismal and deadly hash of British tactics during World War I that the British army was described as "lions led by donkeys," offered this comment on the book:

> Some enthusiasts today talk about the probability of the horse becoming extinct and prophesy that the aeroplane, the tank and the motor-car will supersede the horse in future wars. I believe that the value of the horse and the opportunity for the horse in the future are likely to be as great as ever. . . . I am all for using aeroplanes and tanks, but they are only accessories to the man and the horse.[12]

By 1926 the whole world had accepted the utility of tanks. There is even a record of a group of moonshiners in southern Illinois, the Shelton gang, constructing an armored vehicle for a fight with a band of rival bootleggers. The only place the value of tanks was still in question was in some of the world's top militaries, where the addiction to cavalry still held sway.

By 1929 the British army was spending almost nine times as much for fodder as for gasoline. By 1935 this ratio had decreased to four to one, although by that time Field Marshall Archibald Montgomery-Massingberd had decreed that even tank officers should be provided with horses. For what reason we may only guess.

In 1939 the chickens started coming home to roost. Germany invaded Poland, which had twelve large cavalry brigades that they thought would be able to stop a tank offensive. The brigades lasted less than a month against the German Blitzkrieg, which combined the new technologies of war, the tank and the airplane, to brutal effect. The French lasted only hours against the forces directed by Guderian, the German who studied the writings of British tacticians who had been ignored at home. This stunning success finally put an end to the idea that horses had a place on the modern battlefield and to any lingering suspicions that tanks might not.

This example again shows the effect of prolonged success in creating a mind-set that is invulnerable to change. It also showcases the ability of myth-holders to focus on minor bits of data, such as the Hagler-Ultra bullet, that seem to support their case while ignoring a vast body of evidence that does not.

The way in which several proponents of mechanized warfare were treated also shows the behavior of attacking the nonbeliever. This is something that was not apparent in the Keech case, but the history of religion provides it in ample measure if you look for it. At least the British generals did not put hot irons and thumbscrews on the heretics.

Why are military organizations so prone to mythical thinking? Part of it is understandable. If you are going into a situation where someone is trying to kill you, most of us would do so with a weapon we have used before and we know works, rather than a new one that might be a little better but might flop completely. But the more important reason is the way power is distributed in a military environment. Any military is a top-down organization, and since it is a bureaucracy, you get to the top with age and by not upsetting anyone, especially anyone above you. In addition, when a country is militarily successful, as Britain was, it tends to spend more time at peace, or at least with only minor conflicts. This means that there is little opportunity to test new theories and weapons and provide the objective data that is necessary to explode a myth.

Business Myths

Horrific examples of mythical thinking are actually a bit less common in the business world than they are in the military, religious, or governmental institutions. We have already seen that one of the factors that allow a myth to flourish is an absence of hard data to the contrary. A military organization is not always at war; there is a major conflict every few years and, in between, long periods of inactivity where combat capabilities are secondary to political skills. Hard, disconfirming evidence is hard to come by in this environment.

Modern business, however, runs on quarterly results, and once one quarter's numbers are out of the way, it is time to start worrying about the next. If performance is poor, thus disconfirming management's theories, individual investors begin moving their money out of the company's stock. Large institutional investors, the kind who have seats on the board of directors, start having quiet conversations about whether current management is capable of dealing with the challenges facing the company. Management knows this and is generally ahead of the investors, or at least tries to be. This is not to say that mythical thinking does not go on in the commercial world, it does. But many cases at the highest levels are caught by the investors and don't really get to run their course to destruction.

There are exceptions to this, however, especially when a company has been successful for a long time. When such a company falls from a great height, it tends to hit the ground hard. As an example, let's look at Long-Term Capital Management's fall from dominance in the 1990s.

But first we should call attention to a myth that will play a big role in the business cases, and which we have already seen. While the British military was afflicted with myths about the value of horses, there was another, higher-order myth in play also. This is the myth of "we are the best." This myth is responsible for the most spectacular instances of failure due to mythical thinking, especially in the commercial world.

The sequence runs something like this: An organization is very successful at something; generally it has some unique expertise or skill. Perhaps this organization is extremely innovative and constantly coming up with new products, or perhaps it is very good at watching the details of the production process and driving cost down and product quality up. Whatever it is, there is something the organization does very well, and it has been rewarded for it. The company may be so dominant in the market that it can perform poorly for some time before anyone starts to notice.

In short, the company becomes complacent. The difficult and unsavory tasks don't get done. People who don't perform are retained, and inefficient work processes are left in place simply because fixing the problem is hard work and the company is doing so well that there is no real reason to take on something unpleasant. Leaders begin to preside over kingdoms instead of leading their organizations. This complacent confidence also leads the company to turn inward; after all, if we are the best, why should we listen to anyone else? In this way the company loses touch with its customers and stops watching its competitors.

Swiss Watch Industry

It used to be that something working perfectly was said to "run like a Swiss watch." We don't say that today, primarily because the electronic watch, most often made in Asia, has largely supplanted the perfect mechanical watch that the Swiss excelled at making. But once the Swiss were the 500-pound gorillas of watchmaking.

The industry got its start in Geneva in the mid-1500s when Calvinist reforms banned the wearing of jewels. These rules forced the goldsmiths and jewelers of the city to find a new source of income, and they turned to watchmaking. The Swiss got off to a fast start and for 400 years had no reason to look back. They innovated constantly in both the watch design, introducing the first self-winding watches, for instance, and in manufacturing, being the first to apply mass production to watchmaking.

Before World War II, 90 percent of the watches in the world were made in Switzerland. Even by 1968 the Swiss retained about 65 percent of the watch market and over 80 percent of the profit. By the early 1970s the Swiss watch industry employed over 90,000 people and exported 84 million watches per year.

In 1967 a Swiss research center, the Centre Electronique Horloger, developed the first quartz wristwatch, the Beta 21. Quartz watches keep better time than their mechanical competitors, need less service, are cheaper to make, and do not need winding. Not only did the world's leading watchmakers decide not to pursue the quartz watch, they thought so little of it that they showed it to the world at the 1967 World Watch Congress.

The Japanese, always on the lookout for this kind of mistake, were a bit quicker on the uptake. They mounted a typically Japanese mass assault on the watch industry using the new technology and concentrating on the mass market, where their skills at manufacturing were most applicable.

The Swiss barely knew the fight was on before they were reeling. By 1980 their market share was down to 20 percent, and they employed only 50,000 people; by 1984 this number had stabilized at around 30,000.

The Swiss, to their credit, hung on tenaciously to the upper end of the market, where the mechanics of timekeeping are less important than the art of the jeweler. Today they make more watches in dollar terms than any other country, despite producing only a fraction of the number of timepieces made by Japan and Hong Kong.

The myth here is the same one the British held: "We have been the best in the world for years doing it this way and that thing doesn't even look like a proper (fill in the blank: ship, horse, watch) anyway." It is something we are all prey to.

The quartz watch did not require the kind of precision craftsmanship that the Swiss prided themselves on. It did not have the tiny cams, springs, and rods that defined a watch to people who were justifiably proud of their ability to make such things. Thus, it was not a real watch, and could be exhibited to the world as a curiosity.

If any case illustrates the pernicious effect of prolonged success, it is this one. It also prompts the question of what a successful group is to do. To answer this we need to look more deeply at how success renders an organization myth-bound and how some of them come out of it.

The combination of this case and the British tank saga yields some wisdom. The British had a group of homegrown experts who championed tanks, the Swiss had the developers of the electronic watch. Neither group could convince its power structure to implement the new technology. Why was this?

Part of the problem at the root of these failures is in the makeup of the decision-making groups. In both cases they were homogeneous, made up of groups of people with the same background and experience. Rather than having ten people involved in a decision and thus getting ten brains working on the problem, these groups had the same brain working on it ten times and thus got the same answer over and over again.

The other part of the answer is simply that success discourages innovation. The unsuccessful Germans embraced the tank; the Japanese, at that time just developing as an economic power, took to the electronic watch. In each case success convinced the organization's decision makers that their victories were based on a fundamental truth that could never change: horses and precision craftsmanship in these cases. When the world did change, there was no room for it in the myth.

Long-Term Capital Management

There is no greater documentation that one is a smart person than a Nobel Prize. This highest of honors is reserved for those who have made true, original contributions that outstrip those of their peers. Long-Term Capital Management (LTCM), an investment company, had two Nobel Prize winners among its partners and was widely hailed for its wonderful performance when it crashed and had to be bailed out by a group of large banks. The partners, some of whom had been worth hundreds of millions of dollars, were all but bankrupted.

LTCM had as auspicious a birth as a company can have. It was the creation of J. M. Meriwether, a former bond-trading superstar from Salomon Brothers. He was mathematically talented, which made him a natural for bond trading. Trading bonds and trading stocks are fairly different occupations. When you buy a stock, you buy ownership of the company, and whatever happens to the company happens to you. If it does well, you do well; if it does poorly, so do you. The direction of the stock market is notoriously hard to predict. It depends on all manner of unknowable factors acting together to form a chaotic soup that is difficult to see through.

Bonds, however, are much more predictable. When you buy a bond, you buy debt. The issuer of the bond is bound to repay you, whether the issuer's business is good or not. That said, there are a still a lot of things that go into the value of a bond, the biggest being its risk level. U.S. government bonds, for example, are considered to be virtually risk free. The odds that the United States will be unable to pay its debts are so small that they don't bear consideration. However, some bonds issued by small, risky businesses have a very real risk of not paying out at all; this may happen, for instance, if the company goes bankrupt. Thus these bonds are of more interest to the bondholder than U.S. government bonds. When Meriwether came to Salomon, the bond world was just getting exciting, and eventually he founded and led Salomon's arbitrage group, which would trade in bonds using the company's own money rather than buying and selling bonds for clients.

Meriwether bragged on occasion that he never hired anyone who wasn't smarter than he was, and he seemed to do his best to live up to that motto. In addition, once he hired someone, he trusted that person. On one occasion, when a trader came to him looking for permission to put more money in a trade that was doing poorly, Meriwether gave it to him quickly. When the trader asked whether he wanted to know more about the trade, he replied, "My trade was when I hired you."[13] This kind of faith created intense loyalty in his subordinates; it was also one of the contributors to LTCM's eventual fall.

Among the people Meriwether hired at Salomon were some extremely intelligent individuals. Eric Rosenfeld was an assistant professor at Harvard who didn't enjoy teaching finance. Gregory Hawkins was an MIT finance Ph.D. who had once run Bill Clinton's campaign for attorney general in Arkansas. Victor Haghani had a finance degree from the London School of Economics, and Lawrence Hilibrand, another MIT Ph.D., came to the arbitrage group from Salomon's research department. Meriwether's group was close-knit and secretive; its members socialized primarily among themselves and irritated other traders by refusing to share their methods and data.

Hilibrand was to be an important individual in the events to come. A scrupulously honest "straight arrow" with libertarian political leanings, he fit into the cowboy culture of bond trading even less well than the rest of the professors. Hilibrand was noted for his complete, boundless faith in the predictions of his computer models, and time and again he was right. He traded with scientific precision. While other traders would sweat and worry about a position, he seemed imperturbable. He was so convinced that the markets had to behave according to certain principles that he was not subject to the normal uncertainties of the job. In Hilibrand's time at Salomon, it is rumored that he suffered only a single permanent loss on a trade, an unusual feat.

This band of young geniuses put together computer models that told them when the price of a bond was not behaving as it should, and they were extremely successful. In fact, it seemed like they could do no wrong. The group made money hand over fist for Salomon—over $500 million a year, accounting for most of the company's profits, until Meriwether left in 1991, and continued to do so even after Meriwether was gone and many of his team had followed him to his new company, LTCM, in 1993. Note that these individuals had very similar backgrounds: They were highly trained economists with extensive academic backgrounds. Many had worked together before joining LTCM. This lack of diversity of thinking is common in situations where mythical thinking leads to error.

Salomon, as LTCM would do later, specialized in "convergence trades." In these types of trades, the firm selects two bonds or bond-related securities whose prices seem to be farther apart than they should be. By a series of trades that can be mind-numbingly complex, the firm bets that the lower-priced item will rise and the higher-priced one will fall. If both rise they are protected, and if both fall they are safe, since in each case the money lost on one bet is offset by the gain in the other. If the spread between the instruments closes the firm makes money, and if it opens farther they lose money. In general, these types of trades are based on the idea that the market is not correctly valuing the bonds and that as it becomes more "rational," the gap would close. This belief in the eventual rationality of markets was a cornerstone of the worldview of the partners in LTCM, and they were right. What they failed to consider, however, was whether the market could remain irrational so long that you could go bankrupt waiting for it to come to its senses. You typically don't make much money in convergence trades, so you have to do it big, taking huge positions in the securities. This requires a lot of capital. You may only make a few tenths of a cent on the dollar, but if you invest $1 billion you can do all right. Of course, you also get hit hard.

When Meriwether left Salomon he created LTCM as his vehicle to get back into the game. LTCM was to be a creature known as a hedge fund. Hedge funds are investment funds that are limited in size and typically do business with a small number of wealthy and sophisticated clients. Because of this they are not required to follow the same rules of operation and disclosure as larger mutual funds. The rationale is that the millionaires and large institutional investors can look out for themselves.

LTCM needed several things to get started. First it needed people. Meriwether recruited an all-star cast for his new firm, taking all the superstars named above from the Salomon arbitrage group and adding a few new megastars on top of them, including David W. Mullins, vice chairman of the Federal Reserve, and the number-two man there behind Chairman Alan Greenspan. The biggest names in the new all-star cast, however, were Robert Merton and Myron Scholes. They, along with Fisher Black, would be awarded the Nobel Prize in economics in 1997 for developing the formula for pricing a stock option. Many Wall Street bankers had been trained in the Black-Scholes model in school, and this gave the new firm great credibility. Such was Merton's impact on finance that, years later, Stan Jonas, a derivatives specialist, could say: "Most everything else in finance has been a footnote on what Merton did in the 1970s."[14]

Merton and Scholes did not lead the new firm and did not even act as traders themselves, but they were the intellectual godfathers of the company. In fact, they were among the worldwide leaders of the "efficient market" economists, a group to which most of the other partners belonged. According to the efficient market hypothesis, all the important information about a security is out in the market and already taken into account in the price of the instrument. Thus, it is impossible to beat the market with any regularity because everybody else is just as smart as you are. Since nobody can predict what the effect of new information will be on price, the motion of the stock's price will be random. Some securities will have extremely jumpy prices and others will move around much less, but they will all be unpredictable. This jumpiness is called the volatility of the security, and it is a key element in determining its correct price.

It may sound surprising, especially after our discussion earlier on financial euphoria and the dot.com debacle, but most markets actually are pretty efficient most of the time. The bond market in particular seems to generally obey the efficient market hypothesis pretty well. But being efficient most of the time is not the same as being efficient all the time. The efficient market hypothesis assumes that traders are rational individuals seeking to maximize their own wealth. As we saw in the section on financial euphoria, however, at times large groups of traders can act irrationally. Efficient market theory does not take this fact into account. Of course, some people seem to be able to make good bets on the market. One of these is investor Warren Buffet. Buffet, one of the nation's most widely admired investors, once stated (in Berkshire Hathaway's 1985 annual report) that he should endow a chair at a prestigious university to teach the efficient market hypothesis. In Buffet's words: "What could be more advantageous in an intellectual contest—whether it be bridge, chess or stock selection—than to have opponents who have been taught that thinking is a waste of energy."

The LTCM traders had a bone-deep belief in efficient markets, and it generally served them well. It was not wrong; they just came to believe in it too completely. This is the myth that brought down LTCM, despite the stunning intelligence of its brain trust.

The second thing that Meriwether needed for his new fund was customers. He set out with the unheard-of goal of getting $2.5 billion in investments for his company to manage. Most new funds start with $20 or $30 million. But Meriwether's work at Salomon was known, and the immense credibility of having Merton and Scholes on the team also contributed. Eventually the group was able to raise $1.25 billion, less than Meriwether wanted, but a huge sum.

The last thing necessary was credit, and here again the credibility of the team produced great results. The banking industry fell all over itself to lend money to LTCM at absurdly favorable terms. Every bank thought that if it could build a good relationship with the new firm, it would eventually get to see inside the magic LTCM box and gain great investment insight into the market itself. Eventually LTCM was buying and selling with twenty-eight borrowed dollars for every one of its own, an extremely high ratio and one that would have spooked the banks had they been aware of it.

But for the most part the business world expected great things from the new company. *Business Week* wrote: "Never has this much academic talent been given this much money to play with."[15]

Such were the high expectations for LTCM that it was able to place unusual demands on its investors. The firm would take 25 percent of all gains, compared to a norm of 20 percent, plus 2 percent of all invested capital every year. In addition, investors had to agree to leave their money with LTCM for three years in order to be allowed to invest.

At first the high hopes the investment community had for the new firm seemed to be coming true. In 1994 LTCM made a 28 percent profit on its invested capital, and the investors got 20 percent after LTCM's fees. But better was to come. In 1995 the company made 59 percent on its trades, with investors getting 43 percent. In 1996 the firm made 57 percent and the investors got 41 percent. This was the second myth that hurt LTCM. As described earlier, success breeds the myth of invulnerability, which appears to be what happened at LTCM.

These were wonderful returns for any fund, and it was clear that the partners at LTCM were very good at what they did. Specifically, they were very good at finding risks that were mispriced and then finding a trade that could isolate only that risk and hedge it, so that the firm was not exposed to any more jeopardy than necessary. In the early days, they were generally cautious and very concerned with managing the risk to the firm.

Even in the early days, however, LTCM—mostly Hilibrand and Haghani—had a tendency to make huge trades. With so much capital and leverage, they were able to take billion-dollar positions if they felt they were warranted, and they had the confidence to do so. It is not wrong to make a big bet in the financial world, but you have to be aware that when you do, you might have trouble getting out of it. If I buy a million size 10 sneakers in the expectation that the price will go up, and it goes down instead, I am not going to find anyone who will take that many shoes off my hands, even at a good price. If I had bought only a dozen, it would have been easy to unload them. Eventually LTCM would get caught in a similar situation.

As LTMC's confidence increased, there began to be signs that it had grown too much. David Pflug, head of Global Credit at Chase Manhattan, commented on the Greek letter–filled equations that LTCM used to run its business at one point when LTCM was badgering him for more credit than he thought wise. Pflug said: "You can over intellectualize these Greek letters, one Greek word that ought to be in there is hubris."[16]

By this time the partners were all rich men, worth tens, even hundreds of millions, and they completely believed in what they were doing to such an extent that most of them had their own money invested with the firm. This is an area where the LTCM case is very different from many other such disasters. When Enron failed, it was discovered that high-ranking executives had sold their stock in the company just before it imploded. There was no such activity at LTCM. The partners may have been arrogant and hard-nosed, but they were honest.

By 1997 the firm was an unmitigated success, but the free market punishes success by creating imitators. LTCM was no longer finding pickings quite as rich in the bond markets as it once had; others were playing the same game now, and with a huge capital base it needed to invest it started to look for other places to put its money.

In late 1997 the Nobel for Merton and Scholes was announced, but by this time the two academics were concerned about the fund. They could see that it was getting away from what it knew. The company finished 1997 with a 25 percent return, 17 percent for the investors. The earnings were less than in previous years, but still very good. However, the party was almost over.

Hilibrand and Haghani seemed to be losing the cautious, scientific approach that had made them successful in the first place, or perhaps they were so used to winning in the bond game that they thought they could win at anything, like a chess master who looks at a checkerboard and decides that the game can't be that different from what he's used to. They made bets outside their areas of expertise and seemed to have lost any caution about holding too much of a particular security. Scholes, Merton, and Mullins, three guys everyone should have known better than to ignore, protested, but the inner circle was dominated by the star traders and the trades went forward. At this point the firm had a mind-boggling $134 billion in assets and a great track record; it must have seemed impossible for things to go wrong.

In particular, LTCM seemed to misjudge the market in terms of volatility. Volatility is the "jumpiness" of the market, how much variation there is in the price of securities. The price of an option on a stock (the ability to buy the stock at a preset "strike price") goes up with the volatility of the stock, since a jumpy stock is more likely to hit the strike price as it bounces around. In early 1998 LTCM believed that the market was overvaluing volatility, meaning that the market was not as volatile as many investors believed. This meant that LTCM could sell options at prices that were higher than the true volatility of the market would suggest. Its traders did this with a vengeance. Being believers in efficient markets, they naturally figured that this irrationality would eventually work its way out of the market as people got smarter and things calmed down.

LTCM also took a large position in Russian bonds, apparently for no good reason other than that they were cheap because a lot of people were nervous about the Russian economy and were worried about a default. Here the partners seemed to have bought into the simplistic rationale that was going around Wall Street: that "nuclear powers do not default."

Well, the Russians did default, which set off a panic in the markets, and the Clinton-Lewinsky fiasco in the United States contributed to the market uncertainty. The markets had been in this kind of state before, of course, as recently as 1987, but LTCM's models did not go back that far. Not only did LTCM lose on the Russian bonds, but also as the markets got jittery about the Russian problem, which was spreading to the rest of Asia, stocks started bouncing around; in effect, the volatility of the market increased. Thus many of the options that LTCM had sold reached their strike prices and lost more money for the firm.

Besides this, the general market panic sent investors in search of the most risk-free securities they could find. This wrecked havoc on LTCM's convergence plays by driving the price of low-risk bonds up and widening the spreads between the bonds that LTCM had bet on to converge.

On Friday, August 21, 1998, LTCM lost $553 million—this after the professors had calculated that the largest loss likely in a single day was $35 million. For the year it was already down $1.8 billion.

LTCM was losing tens of millions of dollars a day, but there seemed to be no way out. Meriwether went looking for more investors, but the large, savvy players, like Buffet, generally wanted no part of this game, at least not on terms that LTCM was willing to accept. Eventually, frightened that a failure the size of LTCM would result in a true market meltdown, the Federal Reserve put together a bailout of LTCM in which a group of large banks ponied up several billion dollars in exchange for a 90 percent share in the fund. LTCM's wild ride was over.

The partners, some of whom had been immensely wealthy, were essentially bankrupt. They kept their jobs and their big houses but would never again be "players." The firm's employees also took a beating. Many had most of their own assets invested and lost heavily.

After the fall, the partners did not seem to realize the mistakes they made. They wanted to write their crash off to a once-in-a-lifetime storm of market irrationality that could not reasonably have been expected. This is consistent with other examples of mythical thinking we have seen. The disconfirming evidence is acknowledged in only the smallest possible way. There are three myths here:

1. The almost religious belief in the economic theory of efficient markets

2. The belief that since we have been successful in the past we must be infallible (This belief in infallibility is epidemic in the commercial world.)

3. A close review of commercial decision-making debacles reveals that many have their roots in previous success, which generates myths regarding what works and how business should be done.

NOTES

1. David Perkins, *Outsmarting IQ: The Emerging Science of Learnable Intelligence* (New York: The Free Press, 1995).

2. L. Festinger, H. W. Riecken, and S. S. Schacter, *When Prophecy Fails: A Social and Psychological Study of a Modern Group that Predicted the Destruction of the World* (New York: Harper Torchbooks, 1956).

3. David Divine, *The Blunted Sword* (London: Hutchinson & Co., 1964), and Norman Dixon, *On the Psychology of Military Incompetence* (London: Jonathan Cape Ltd., 1976).

4. David Divine, *The Blunted Sword* (London: Hutchinson & Co., 1964).

5. Ibid.

6. Norman Dixon, *On the Psychology of Military Incompetence* (London: Jonathan Cape Ltd., 1976).

7. Ibid.

8. Bryan Cooper, *The Ironclads of Cambrai* (London: Souvenir Press, 1967).

9. Winston Churchill, *The World Crisis* (New York: Scribner, 1955).

10. David Divine, *The Blunted Sword* (London: Hutchinson & Co., 1964).

11. Liddell Hart, *Paris, or the Future of War* (New York: Dutton, 1925).

12. David Divine, *The Blunted Sword* (London: Hutchinson & Co., 1964).

13. Roger Lowenstein, *When Genius Failed* (New York: Random House, 2000).

14. Ibid.

15. Ibid.

16. Ibid.

Tribal Thinking

Tribal thinking means allowing our relationships with others to keep us from thinking about a situation correctly. We are social animals, and we value our standing in the tribe. Those of our ancestors who were valued and respected in the tribe were able to live longer and better, mate more often, and in general pass on their genes more frequently. A man who helped a woman in a moment of need probably increased his chances of passing on his genes. Those who could not work and play well with others tended to get kicked out of the tribe, where they likely starved or were eaten.

Our place in the group is important to us. Someone who attempts to speak against the group consensus might be ignored and her place in the group questioned. A man who displays "good tribe member" behavior improves his chances of passing his genes on to the next generation, assuming a hostile tribal member doesn't kill him first.

It is not only natural for human beings to think tribally, it is necessary. We don't have teeth or claws or even a proper snout to bite with; we can't run fast and we don't have a shell to hide in. Our Paleolithic ancestors had three things going for them: opposable thumbs, devious brains, and the fact that they could work together. Staking out your own little bit of the jungle and driving everybody else away except at mating time is fine, if you are a tiger, but for a hairless ape, it's suicide.

In general, this chapter deals with cases that include one of four types of error, all related to group membership and function:

1. **Tribal-centricity.** Excessive regard for the in-group and disdain for others. In this form the in-group is considered superior to others. It is

the high-school clique writ large. Abilities and characteristics of the in-group are considered superior to others, sometimes leading to overconfidence in group decision making, as illustrated by the illusion of invulnerability we will see in the Bay of Pigs case. This behavior is also shown in the way people can be induced to buy things from people with whom they share membership in some group. This "tribal marketing" is a special application of tribal thinking and is shown in a later case.

Closely related to excessive regard for the in-group is its opposite. In this case the abilities and value of groups other than our own are underestimated, leading to misjudgments about them. The military cases, such as Isandhwala, show this phenomenon clearly, as does the not-invented-here syndrome, which appears in many environments but is easiest to find in the commercial world.

2. **Inability to challenge an apparent group consensus.** We will see this most strongly in the Bay of Pigs case, where concern for group harmony precluded good debate on options regarding Cuba. When groups of people meet to work together, they can get so caught up in their own group membership that they refuse to do anything that could disrupt the group, such as disagree with a fellow member. This is most common in situations where the group is new and the members are still trying to feel one another out and want to avoid making enemies.

3. **Following the group.** The management fads case to be described illustrates this phenomenon very well, as does every other fad that has ever existed. When we see other people doing something, we assume it must be a good idea. Unfortunately the other guy might be just as ignorant as we are. This concept showed up in a weaker form in the Bay of Pigs case, where President Kennedy's advisors seemed to be under the impression that everyone else was in favor of the plan and therefore decided that it must be the right thing to do.

4. **Monolithic group membership.** Sometimes tribal thought flourishes when all members of the group have a similar background. When diagnosing a problem in a commercial organization, it's common to find out that every person on the team that is making mistakes has basically the same resume. In effect, there is nobody to

challenge the tribal thinking as it emerges. Incidentally, it also means that the team may not have all the skills it needs to solve the problem.

SCIENCE

One of the most vivid illustrations of tribal thought in the laboratory is provided by a set of experiments conducted in the 1950s.[1] In these experiments, the investigators showed a group of individuals a line, along with two or three other lines for comparison. The experimenters then asked the members of the group, one at a time, to tell them which of the comparison lines was the same length as the first line. The trick here was that in each group, only one person was the subject of the experiment. All the rest were accomplices of the experimenter. The chairs were always arranged so that the true subject gave his or her opinion last, and the accomplices were coached ahead of time on what their response should be. In all cases it was obvious which line was identical, and when the judgments were made in private, they were always accurate. But when they were made in public, it was a different story. In a third of the cases, the accomplices gave the right answer and the subjects did the same; but the other two thirds of the time, the accomplices were told to say that another, obviously incorrect, line was the identical one. The investigators found that subjects would conform to the majority view about 30 percent of the time and give the obviously incorrect answer. Also, about 60 percent of the subjects conformed to the majority view on at least one trial. The original goal of these experiments had been to study independence, but when the experimenters saw the results, they quickly changed the focus to conformity and ended up with one of the most cited experiments in this area of study.

It is fairly easy to see the real-world application of these experiments. You are in a meeting where everyone else seems to have a certain viewpoint. Even though you think their approach is probably wrong, you yield to the collective wisdom of the group. Among our ancestors, those who bucked the group had less chance of surviving, so the conformists bred more often and passed their genes down to us.

In an interesting extension of this experiment, investigators used much the same approach, but in each group only a minority—two out of five—of the participants were in league with the experimenter.[2] In this case the participants were asked to name the color of a blue slide. When the accomplices stated that the slide was green instead of blue, they were able to get about 10 percent of the subjects to go along with them. Granted this is a minority, but many decisions in the real world hinge on getting 10 percent of a group to change its mind. Also, in this experiment the accomplices were not allowed to argue vigorously for their opinion, as sometimes happens in the real world. Thus it won't be a surprise when we see cases where a minority was able to hijack a group of sharp people into a dumb decision. Both of these studies have results that we might have expected. After all, we know that people like to follow the group, so while the percentages might be a surprise, the fact that some people will make a clearly incorrect call if everyone else does should not be a total surprise.

Another set of experiments shows an even stranger result in this area, called "group polarization."[3] Researchers kind of stumbled onto this phenomenon in the early 1960s. Many decisions involve trading off risk and reward, such as deciding whether to take a job at a new dot.com, where the risks are high but the potential rewards are great, or at an established company, where you are less likely to be fired within the week. At the time of these experiments, people thought that group decisions were generally more cautious than individual decisions. This idea makes a certain amount of sense since the group will have to persuade its most cautious member to go along with whatever decision is proposed; thus the group could be expected to be fairly risk-averse. What the experiment found was just the opposite, however. Group decisions and individual opinions seemed to get riskier after group discussion. Initially this was known as a risky-shift.

After decades of research we now know that this is a bit of a misnomer. Groups don't make people seek risk, but they do induce people to make more extreme decisions in whatever direction they were inclined to lean in the first place. There are a number of theories as to why this happens. Some researchers think it is a matter of the group members trying to show that they have qualities that society approves of. If society likes risk-taking adventurers, then people in groups try to look more this way, or adjust their behavior so their self-image can remain more adventurous than that of the next person. Personally, I like the theory that says that people shift farther in the direction the group already leans because the group is better able to produce arguments for that side, which of course group members find persuasive. This experiment shows how group dynamics can influence our thinking unconsciously, even if we are scrupulously fair about not letting ourselves be swayed by blatant majority pressure.

Another study showed the power of the drive to go along with the group by looking at jury behavior. It found that hung juries are more likely when jurors vote by a show of hands than when a secret ballot is used. This is consistent with the idea that once we have made a public statement to the tribe, we find it difficult to change. It also demonstrates how tribal considerations can reinforce mythical thinking. The commitment made in a public vote is rendered much more powerful when we know that the rest of the tribe has seen it and is expecting us to act in accordance with it.

Cases

Racial Superiority: White Supremacy

Race is perhaps the ultimate tribe. Most peoples have creation myths that set them apart from everyone else. Here is one from the Philippines:

> God carefully shapes a small clay figure but does not know how much heat is needed to bake it. Left too long in the oven, the image comes out burned black. This is the Negro. The next figure is under baked and comes out pasty white. The Caucasian. The third time God takes his clay from the oven at exactly the right moment, when it is a lovely warm brown. So the brown man, the Malay and Filipino, begins his career by pleasing God.[4]

But what is race? The American Anthropological Association says this in its "Statement on Race," which is available on its Web site at www.aaanet.org/stmts/racepp.htm:

> Evidence from the analysis of genetics (e.g., DNA) indicates that most physical variation, about 94%, lies within so-called racial groups. Conventional geographic "racial" groupings differ from one another only in about 6% of their genes. This means that there is greater variation within "racial" groups than between them. . . . whenever different groups have come into contact, they have interbred. The continued sharing of genetic materials has maintained all of humankind as a single species.

So race is a fairly muddled concept, and differences between races are fairly small genetically. The statement continues:

> From its inception, this modern concept of "race" was modeled after an ancient theorem of the Great Chain of Being, which posited natural categories on a hierarchy established by God or nature. It subsumed a growing ideology of inequality devised to rationalize European attitudes and treatment of the conquered and enslaved peoples. Proponents of slavery in particular during the 19th century used "race" to justify the retention of slavery.

Believers in the concept of "white supremacy" often have tried to find its basis in Christian scripture. Before 1500 or so, people believed in the "Hametic curse." As described in the first chapter of Genesis in the Bible, Noah had three sons, Shem, Ham, and Japeth. Noah was apparently an enterprising individual; besides saving the world's creatures from death in the flood, he was also the first man to make wine. One evening, after some overenthusiastic experimentation with his new creation, Noah fell into a drunken sleep, naked (although the Bible makes no mention of what happened to his clothes). Ham saw him in this state and instead of covering him up went and told his brothers, who threw a cloak over him. When Noah awoke he was in an understandably bad mood, upset at having been seen in such a state, and probably hung over as well. He blamed Ham for his humiliation and cursed Ham's son, Canaan, making him a slave; this is the "Hametic curse."

European scholars believed that this curse justified making the descendants of Ham slaves forever. Blacks were thus assumed to have descended from Ham, whites from Japeth, and Asians from Shem. As late as 1861 Jefferson Davis, the president of the Confederate States during the U.S. Civil War, claimed that "slavery was established by decree of Almighty God. . . . it is sanctioned in the Bible, in both testaments, from Genesis to Revelation."[5]

Such is the foolishness men undertake when convinced they know the mind of God.

Thus, the idea of being God's best-loved race isn't unique to the Filipinos. The literature of white supremacy consistently attempts to gain scriptural backing for its beliefs. But if there is one thing you can say for the philosophy of white superiority, it is that it has a perverse diversity. There are almost as many versions of how the world came to be and why white people are superior as there are writers on the subject.

One school of thought says that all humans are descended from Adam, who was white, and that blacks and other races drifted away from whites and degenerated through the centuries until they were clearly inferior. A variation on that theme is that whites evolved, but other races did not; this belief gets to the same place, white superiority, but by a different path.

What is interesting to the casual observer is that none of these alternative histories can be justified by scripture, so not only are those who believe in these ideas laying aside the science, but they are also ignoring their own holy writ.

White superiority also looks to history for justification, and it is here that we can point out its greatest logical problems. The logic runs something like this: Aryans, a people from western Asia and the original speakers of the Indo-European root language, are the paragons of humanity, as evidenced by their ability to conquer everyone else, as they did in India, Africa, and the Middle East, and the fact that they are perfect specimens of blond, blue-eyed beauty. The most perfect expression of the Aryan race today can be found in the Western European Germanic bloodline or in the WASP (white, Anglo-Saxon Protestant) founders of America. This bloodline is being steadily diluted by lesser races, possibly as part of a plan by the world's Jews to destroy the superior Aryans.

This line of thought gives the Aryans credit for creating almost every advance in the history of humanity. Civilizations as far removed as India and the New World were all supposedly founded by stray Aryans, although the archaeological evidence supporting such a theory is exactly zero.

I have ancestors from both Germany and Greece, and we know that while the Greeks, along with the Chinese and the Ethiopians, were operating fairly advanced societies, wearing robes, doing trigonometry, and debating philosophy hundreds of years before Christ, the German branch of the family was still running around the forest in fur jock straps and horned hats. History shows that the Germans are a people like any other, no matter how much some folks wish otherwise.

Nowhere does the ability of tribal thought to suppress common sense come through more clearly than in the opinions of white supremacist groups about breeding. Interbreeding is a special irritant for these groups since it dilutes the genes of the superior Aryan race. Here is a passage written by Ben Klassen, founder of the Church of the Creator, a white supremacist group. He is talking about interbreeding between species of swallow and what would happen if the birds didn't know enough to mate only among their own species:

> Then all the species would soon be mongrelized into one mixed-up species. Furthermore, the mongrelized swallow would soon breed with the 75 species of mongrelized larks and we would soon have a swallark. The mongrelized swallark would soon breed with the mongrelized cardinals and bluebirds and the whole process would degenerate into a mongrelized bird. The end result would soon be that birds would lose their own innate, peculiar characteristics that enabled them to survive all these thousands of years.[6]

Presumably the mongrelized birds would then breed with mongrelized turtles, pigs, pine trees, and so forth, until the only life-form left was a mongrelized something, probably sporting wings, gills, antennae, and acorns. Humans are, in this view, the only animal that flouts this law of nature by breeding outside its species.

What Klassen misses here is that swallows and larks are different species and *cannot* interbreed. This is a simple and fundamental law understood by every kid who ever took fifth-grade science, but it is brushed aside by the furor of Klassen's tribal thought.

The white superiority groups in the United States are less homogeneous than most people believe. They are not all Christian Fundamentalist Nazis. Some seem to believe that Christianity, being derived from Judaism, is a "mongrel religion" and prefer a homegrown faith that emphasizes the good of the Aryan race. Many are not supporters of the United States, feeling that the nation is too mongrelized to be saved, and want to start their own country. Some are anticapitalism.

While the level of diversity of thought within the white supremacy groups indicates a bit of intellectual activity, it is kind of like a football game in a closet. There is superficial motion, but the constraining walls are too tight, and it is too dark, to make any real progress. Tied as they are to their notions of race as the measure of all things, and to the belief that might makes right in issues of race, they are forced into beliefs that would strike them as ridiculous if they weren't so blindsided by their uncritical praise of their tribe.

Racial Superiority: Black Supremacy

As a philosophy, white superiority got off to a several-hundred-year head start over black superiority. But in recent years the black superiority crew has made up some time. Black superiority in the United States tends to be based less on religion and more on a kind of New Age pseudoscience and a bizarre history of the world that yields nothing to the white supremacists in terms of fantasy.

Like many of the problems in thinking discussed in this book, the black superiority mind-set has a legitimate beginning. Western scholarship has had a European bias for centuries, which is understandable given that most of the scholars were European or of European ancestry. Beginning in the 1960s African American studies programs were instituted in many universities to help correct this and to represent history more completely. Unfortunately, some of these efforts degenerated into political rather than scholarly activities, and truth, as always, has become a casualty of politics.

The most egregious of the Afrocentric "historians" have mimicked their Aryan counterparts in placing their tribe at the center of every historical advance. At the top of this list is George G. M. James, whose 1954 book *Stolen Legacy* makes the charge that Greek philosophy, the foundation of western civilization, was stolen from Egypt, a black civilization.[7] This claim is a mixture of truth and falsehood. Certainly Greece borrowed from the older civilization in Egypt, but it also created its own knowledge and philosophy, supplementing, extending, and improving on what it got from Egypt.

There is also the question of calling Egypt a "black civilization." For some reason the Afrocentrists have focused especially on Cleopatra in looking for black Egyptians. In fact, she is one of the least likely of Egyptians to have black ancestry. Cleopatra was of Macedonian lineage, a descendant of Ptolemy, one of Alexander the Great's generals. While it is possible that she had some black ancestors, it's a bit unlikely given the rules for breeding in force for royal families at the time, which encouraged incest in order to keep power in the family. In addition, pictures of her found on coins of the era clearly depict her with Mediterranean features.

One of my favorite examples of reducing everything to tribal prejudices is this one from Frances Cress Welsing, whose 1991 book *The Isis Papers: The Keys to the Colors* is as desperate an attempt to racialize the world as one is apt to find, and basically says that everything wrong with the world is due to white fear of genetic extermination.[8] Here is Cress Welsing's statement about how the Christian cross represents the genitals of a castrated black man:

I submit that the cross, as an important and provocative symbol in the white supremacy system/culture, is none other than a brain-computer distillate of the white collective's fear-induced obsession with the genitals of all non-white men (of Black men in particular), who have the potential to genetically annihilate the white race.

A surprise, I'm sure, to the tens of millions of black Christians in America. Cress Welsing believes that white skin is a form of albinism. In fact, albinism is a genetic condition that prevents people from making melanin, and albinos tend to sunburn easily and have vision problems. It is not the same as Caucasian ancestry. Similarly, individuals of Hispanic descent in the United States tend to be a bit shorter than average, but this does not mean that being Mexican is a form of dwarfism. The idea is ridiculous unless you are deep in the grip of tribal thought. I can do no greater justice to Cress Welsing's thoughts on the Christmas tree than to reproduce them: "The Christmas tree is, in its abstracted form, a cross—the symbol of the Black male genitals. First, the Christmas tree is chopped down in the forest. Then it is taken home. In the U.S., when the Christmas tree is decorated 'colored balls' are hung on the tree."

Try as I might, I can't think of anything to add to this.

Melanin is a special fixation of the black superiority movement. Melanin is the skin pigment that makes blacks darker than whites. It is also responsible for tanning of the skin in response to sunlight. Melanin is dark brown, and it has the effect of absorbing ultraviolet light and thus protecting the skin from the rays that can cause skin cancer, which is only one tenth as common in blacks as in whites. A fairly typical view of melanin is this one from the rastafarian.net Web site, rastafarian.net/what_is_melanin.htm:

> The truth about Melanin is up to now a closely kept secret, for Melanin is Blackness itself, that is to say, the single chemical responsible for colouring the skin pigments in black people, melanin is the human's only protection from the natural rays of the sun. It also possesses the unique ability to absorb various energy sources and convert these absorbed energies into re-usable energy, this includes mediums such as: music vibration and sound waves, the sun rays, sun heat, light rays etc.

In this conception, black people are big solar batteries storing up energy in their melanin for later use. Cress Welsing has a similar comment about melanin, claiming that its absence "critically impairs the depth sensitivity of the nervous system and the ability to tune in to the total spectrum of energy frequencies in the universe."[9]

Of course melanin is no such thing. It is a pigment that protects people from overexposure to the sun, nothing more. Cress Welsing, a medical doctor, should understand the lack of a physiological basis for these bizarre claims about melanin, but apparently she is so far in the grip of her tribal paradigm that she cannot.

People like Ben Klassen and Frances Cress Welsing are not stupid; Klassen was an engineer and Cress Welsing a medical doctor. Both write fairly well and on another topic might be perfectly reasonable. But in areas related to their tribes they adopt a willful ignorance that is breathtaking in its scope. I mean that literally; when you read their books, you (or I at least) really do have to set them down occasionally to take a breath and get your mind around the magnitude of the claims.

Disdain for the Enemy

Underestimating the enemy is a bit of tribal thought that has special significance for soldiers. Military organizations are well aware of the dangers of underestimating the enemy, at least today. But avoiding this error can be difficult when the enemy comes from a race or group that is despised, which of course are just the groups one ends up fighting.

Any military needs to be confident. Nobody runs into a fight expecting to get beaten up, and soldiers have to believe that they are going to win. But giving too little credit to the enemy has its costs. Military history provides us with numerous examples of underestimating the enemy and the price it exacts. The American underestimation of the Vietnamese in the twentieth century, the Roman's disdain for the Germans that led to the loss of the legions at Teutoburger Wald in AD 9, all the way back to the overconfidence of the Persians that led to history-changing defeats against the Greeks at Marathon in 490 BC and Salamis in 480 BC all are examples of underestimating an enemy.

In American history, we might think first of George Custer and his disastrous attempt to defeat several thousand rifle-armed Indians with his 675 cavalrymen in 1876. Custer made this idiocy worse by declining reinforcements when they were offered and by dividing his command into three smaller units. But this book is about smart people doing dumb things, and while the individuals featured in the other cases are not all Einsteins, I am drawing the line at Custer. Custer was not a smart guy who made a mistake; he was pathologically indifferent to personal danger, and had shown this during his entire career. The Battle of Little Big Horn was just a case of a guy who kept making the same mistakes until he ran out of luck and got scalped.

This mistake of underestimating the enemy occurs most often when white, technologically advanced colonial powers are fighting against forces they consider beneath them. While this is a common way for the error to occur, it is an oversimplification to think it's the only place this particular misjudgment happens. The urge to underestimate the enemy is much broader than this. In World War II both Hitler and Stalin underestimated their foes at different times, and Robert E. Lee, fighting against other Americans, clearly underestimated his foes at Gettysburg, where he ordered his men to attack an entrenched enemy holding higher ground. Lee later admitted that he was convinced, possibly encouraged, by a recent victory against a larger force at Chancellorsville, that his troops could do anything.

Neither is the error of underestimating the enemy unique to military scenarios. The Japanese economic assault on the U.S. automobile industry is also a case of this error type, at least in part. The men who ran that industry considered themselves the industrial elite of planet Earth. Accepting the idea that Japan could build better cars than America, ship them across the Pacific Ocean, and still sell them cheaper than Detroit was not a compliment they were prepared to extend to the Japanese, especially since "we" had just beaten "them" in another test of industrial and technological might: World War II.

Management Fads: Quality Circles

The case of management fads illustrates a different facet of tribal thinking, the process of going along with what everyone else is doing, as intelligent, educated managers have had a distressing tendency to do in recent years. In this case the tribe is the rest of the commercial world.

The area of management fads probably deserves its own book, not merely its own section. It is one of the most fascinating areas of applied psychology that I know of. It is also one of the most maddening to those who have suffered the impact of management fads and frauds on the workplace.

We rather expect fads in some things. But most of us think that management is too important to leave to fad makers; that by the early twenty-first century we should have figured out how to run a complex business and no longer allow ourselves to be seduced by the management equivalent of pet rocks.

Why should there even be such a thing as a management fad? Why would managers read books like *The Management Secrets of Attila the Hun*? My wife designs water and wastewater facilities, and I have never seen her read a book with a title anything like *The Wastewater Process Equations of Attila the Hun,* yet supposedly management, which is at least as difficult as engineering, can be reduced to this kind of simplistic rubbish. There have been fads for reengineering, total quality management (TQM), teams, self-managed teams, learning organizations, and a mind-bending array of New Age twaddle about empowering people and focusing the "positive energy" of employees. Many of these fads have a core of truth, but it is so buried in jargon intended to make the originator appear smart that it is almost unidentifiable. One reason these things take hold is that management fads are like other fads; they depend on people following along with others without thinking too much.

Peter Drucker, America's foremost management thinker, when asked why American management is so fashion conscious, summarized the problem in this way:

> Insecurity. We've been caught in a period of very rapid change; the feeling is that there must be a right answer. But also, thinking is very hard work. And management fashions are a wonderful substitute for thinking. . . .
>
> Each evangelist is quite sure that his own patent medicine cures everything. And it's very hard to get management to ask, "Is this for us?" There is no universal medicine. The stuff that is good for my arthritis would not help me at all with a broken leg, even though it's in the same general area. . . .
>
> It also, I think, bespeaks a systemic behavior of adolescents. Compared to [managers], a 15 year old is a conservative.[10]

This may sound a bit strange. Most of us are used to thinking of corporate managers as gray-haired, uncreative men who wear belts just in case their suspenders break, but this is not really the case. While conservative in some areas, American management has a bias for action; it wants to do something, not sit and study things. In general this is a wonderful trait, but it has a downside too. Drucker continues:

> They yield to peer pressure. If a fellow CEO on the golf course says, "We are using this, and we wouldn't do without it," you have to do it, too. The last 20 years have been very unsettling. Executives really don't understand the world in which they live. But bandwagon psychology is nothing new. When I was growing up in Vienna, everybody felt the need to be psychoanalyzed. And there was a time when every child older than 4 years had to have his tonsils out. So this is not confined to management.

It seems strange that corporate executives should be making decisions based on what everyone else is doing rather than detailed analysis. But I remember being flabbergasted when I asked an executive what kind of cost-benefit analysis had been done regarding a multi–tens-of-million-dollar computer system he was installing, and he replied "none." It isn't that people think these fads are reliable. Rupert Murdoch, the Australian media tycoon, summed up the attitude of many managers toward the fads and gurus of management: "Guru? You find a gem here or there. But most of it's fairly obvious, you know. You go to Doubleday's business section and you see all these wonderful titles and you spend $300 and then you throw them all away."[11]

By one count, only one out of five popular management books sold is read to completion.[12] I can't think of a more damning statistic. Even more skeptical attitudes are easy to find. When John Micklethwait and Adran Wooldridge wrote their excellent book, *Witchdoctors,* on the guru industry, an editor at *The Economist* said to them:

> You know what worries me about your book about management theory: That you'll talk to all the people and read all the books; that you will detail all its incredible effects—the number of jobs lost, the billions of dollars spent, and so on. And you won't say the obvious thing: that it's 99 percent bullshit. And everybody knows that.[13]

While this probably overstates the situation, at least by a few percent, there is plenty of objective data that managing by fad is not good for your organization. The great management technique of the 1980s was TQM. TQM was an American attempt to duplicate some of the group problem-solving and continuous improvement techniques of the Japanese. It was phenomenally successful in terms of being implemented; everyone seemed to have one of these programs. (In the interest of truth, I must admit to helping implement both TQM and reengineering efforts as a consultant. Like every consultant, I think mine were the good ones.) By 1993 one researcher was able to review a number of studies that looked at the impact of TQM and write: "About one-fifth, and at best one-third of TQM programs in the U.S. and Europe have achieved 'significant' or even 'tangible' improvements in quality, productivity, competitiveness or financial returns."[14]

These are pretty poor results for something that cost as many billions as TQM. The fad of the 1990s was process reengineering, a structured look at the processes by which work is accomplished, and it had similar results, which were even more disappointing due to the ridiculously overblown hype of the people who sold it. Reengineering was going to reverse the Industrial Revolution. At best all it did was improve process efficiency, sometimes at the expense of strategy so that companies became very good at doing things that were not important.

There are many reasons for management fads. For one thing, many of them do have value. Remember, one quarter to one third of the TQM implementations did produce tangible results. This value will be evident when we look in more detail at the quality circle craze of the late 1970s and early 1980s later in this section. The quality circles case is interesting because, even though it was a fad, and even though it did not last, it did contribute to America's understanding of the processes of management.

Other fads have not contributed at all, and some of the New Age material has clearly set the process of management back rather than forward. But often even something that is implemented as a fad and does not live up to its billing eventually does make a contribution. Drucker said this about reengineering: "Reengineering became the bandwagon, and everybody jumped on it. Now many have jumped off. Predictably, there will be a lot of companies that will quietly keep on doing it and then in six years will know how to do it."[15]

Thus, we can say that the basic reason for management fads is the same as for any fad. It is tribal thinking of the follow-the-pack type. But to be fair, fads involve a number of other contributing factors, and we must understand these factors to really know how the tribal aspect operates.

Fads also come into being because, in the management area, there is a lack of solid, documented science and practice that is available in other fields. Engineers learn techniques and equations in school, apply them under supervision as junior contributors, and finally take leadership themselves and instruct others in the correct application of the concepts learned in school. Part of the reason this doesn't work in the area of management is because management science is undeveloped.

The science of management now stands at a point similar to that at which medicine stood in the mid- to late 1800s and where physics was centuries before. It is what you might call a proto-science, something that might someday grow into a science but just isn't there yet. At this stage there are all manner of competing theories and outlooks, none of which has proven to be worth elevating to the status of a general knowledge framework to anchor a science.

Another part of the problem is the result of the poor job that has often been done in management education. But the issue is also deeper than a poor business school curriculum. Management is a difficult subject from which to develop a science. In any experiment there are 100 variables that might not behave the same way if the same thing was attempted again in another situation. When a materials researcher wants to isolate the tensile strength of steel, she simply puts a standard bar of it in a machine and pulls it until it breaks. She has to be a bit aware of the temperature, but that's about it. She does not have to contend with the fact that a particular type of steel in India might have different properties than steel in Indiana. The machine operator is unlikely to implement the experiment incorrectly, and the steel has no reason to be suspicious of the professor and behave strangely. If the industry has a downturn, the steel will not quit to go to work somewhere else or get disgruntled at its compensation package. Most important of all, the researcher can run the experiment 100 times just the same way. In the management world, the scientist has none of these advantages, and thus the science has not evolved as far as its cousins.

Another reason for management fads is that most good managers, as mentioned, are action oriented. They prefer to do something rather than nothing, and if they get it wrong, they assume that they will figure out the problem and get it right next time. Unfortunately, many management solutions take years to bear fruit, and even when the individual is still around for that time, he may lose interest in the technique or simply run out of energy.

Management fads also proliferate because of something of an unholy alliance between academia and the consulting profession, a $20 billion-a-year business even if you use a very restrictive definition. Both groups have a vested interest in finding new ways to manage. Whenever some middle manager in a commercial organization finds a good way to do something, an academic is there to declare that this is a new and significant development, give it a name, and write a book. At this point the consultants take over and the "New Paradigm" is marketed in a slick and vivid way, with the implication that this is the thing that all the smart people are doing and that if you don't do it, you are incompetent. There is a lot of money at stake in this game. American firms now spend more than $15 billion a year on outside advice and consulting, and some gurus get tens of thousands of dollars for a daylong seminar. Clearly, a lot of people have a stake in keeping the management fad industry going.

Implementing a fad gives managers something to say when they're asked what they're doing to improve their area; and the involvement of the consultants and academics legitimizes it. In addition, the fad can help define the organization. One study found that while use of new management techniques did not appear to contribute to the bottom line of companies that used them, the use of cutting-edge management strategies did contribute to a positive reputation for those firms and better chief executive pay. Thus, you might get some payback just in terms of respect, if not improved performance, for using these tactics.

American managers have been through a long list of management techniques, some of which can be called fads and some of which were just reasonable attempts at doing things better. Even a fairly good technique with solid evidence behind it can be implemented in a faddish way; that is, with a short-term perspective and little real commitment to doing what must be done to make it work. Very little happens overnight in a large company. When Jack Welch, an outstanding manager, took over at General Electric (GE), in 1981 he set a goal of improving productivity by 6 percent per year. It was not until 1987, six years later, that GE finally saw productivity jump from 2 percent, where it had been, to 5 percent, and not until 1989 that the 6 percent goal was achieved—despite the best efforts of an excellent manager. Unfortunately, this long lead time for payback on management initiatives makes it hard to track the effectiveness of management techniques. It also means that the perpetrators of an unsuccessful effort, inside and outside the company, probably will not be around when it can be revealed to be successful or unsuccessful. Unfortunately, American industry has been a bit quick—certainly quicker than, say, British industry—to jump on new fads.

It is important to understand the damage that management fads do. It is not just the money spent implementing them and the poor results that they often yield. The most damaging part of a management fad is the destruction it wreaks on the organization. Individual contributors lose any faith they might have had in their management when they see how shallow the fad is. This loss of faith in turn makes it more difficult to implement even the most routine changes that might have been put in place easily before. Talented people leave the organization in droves. After all, nothing is more demotivating and demoralizing than believing that your superiors are incompetent.

The quality circle craze is a typical example of a management fad. The late 1970s and early 1980s were tough times for American managers. The Japanese seemed to be beating them at everything they put their hands to, and the automobile industry in particular was coming under pressure from Europe as well. One reason for this was the issue of "quality," real and perceived.

People have used a number of definitions for quality over the years, but during this period the American and Japanese versions were very different. The American manager's perception of quality centered around the product, and in particular the number of features of the product. A high-quality product meant lots of bells and whistles, especially in the automobile industry, where the fetish for gimmickry was almost completely out of hand (remember the Ford Edsel with its push-button gearshift?).

The Japanese approach was a bit different. For one thing, it included the idea of process quality, meaning that as much emphasis should be placed on the manufacturing process as on the final product so that defect rates would be low, waste minimized, and the final product of generally better mechanical soundness. The Japanese worked the manufacturing process in a much more sophisticated way than the Americans, looking for the root cause of a defect and then changing the process to eliminate it rather than just tightening inspection criteria to improve quality, which is much more expensive.

A good example of this difference can be seen in the way Hewlett-Packard (HP) addressed a quality problem in computer chip production. In 1980 HP found that Japanese 16K DRAM chips had a failure rate of between one sixteenth and one fourteenth that of American chips, depending on the maker. HP set out to address the problem and by 1983 had closed the gap but had not addressed the underlying problem. The quality gain was based mostly on tighter inspection criteria and thus led to higher costs; in addition, in later and more complex chips, the quality gap appeared again.

In general, American management didn't know quite what to do with the issue of quality. Managers don't put their hands on the tools, so how could they be the ones to build better cars? Management tended to blame labor, which did play a role, but certainly did not deserve the complete responsibility some managers assigned to it. Also, a joint venture between General Motors and Toyota demonstrated that American workers could indeed build better-quality cars than predicted when managed correctly, although they did not reach the quality levels achieved in Japan.

There was also data to suggest that the quality gap with the Japanese was more a matter of perception than reality, data that, of course, the Americans clung to like drowning people. The idea of analyzing the manufacturing process for quality was not something they understood. Different industries coped as well as they could. The steel industry looked for political protection, much as it does today, and the auto industry just gave up in the compact end of the market, just as the semiconductor industry ceded the memory chip market to the Japanese. But giving up is not a strategy, and even as they fought to deny reality, American managers also sought solutions. One of these was "quality circles."

Quality circles are small groups of employees from the same work area that meet to solve work problems, generally after work, or over lunch, or some other time that does not take them away from their normal duties. These groups are trained in simple problem-solving techniques and may be rewarded for their efforts in a variety of ways, from bonuses to simple recognition. The technique was used in Japan as part of a much broader quality focus that included manufacturing process analysis and a management culture that valued process quality. Quality circles were also highly customized by each Japanese firm to its particular needs. In Japan quality circles were a significant, but far from the most significant, contributor to quality.

Although they were not a cure-all, quality circles were a very visible part of the Japanese quality effort. When an American group toured a Japanese plant, they saw the circles meeting, presenting their results to upper management, and papering the shop walls with charts showing progress against goals. This view of Japanese quality also played to the American perception that the real problem was the laziness of the workforce. If quality circles were a way to engage line workers so they would do the quality of work that they were capable of, then so be it. Thus it is not surprising that employee meetings and progress charts would be the aspect of Japanese quality management that American firms tried to emulate.

Quality circles first came to America when a Lockheed missile systems manager, Wayne Rieker, saw a presentation by a visiting Japanese group. Rieker put together a trip to Japan to study the technique and implemented quality circles in 1974. By 1977 the company could claim millions of dollars in savings, and the movement was off and running. By 1982, 44 percent of all companies with over 500 employees had quality circles, and by 1984, about 90 percent of the Fortune 500 had the program in place. Robert Cole, a thoughtful observer of this period, had this to say:

> There was an enormous bandwagon effect as the quality circle fad took hold; companies adopted them because it was the thing to do, and their domestic competitors were doing it, and the Japanese were doing it, and the media were telling them they were backward if they did not do it. Clearly this environment did not encourage cool, deliberative thought about the firm's strategic choices.[16]

Quality circles seemed like the perfect quality tool. They were easy to understand and implement, they did not demand large reorganizations or that managers change cherished mind-sets. Consulting firms sprang up to help put them in place, often led by individuals whose only credential was that they'd assisted in implementing the tool at another American firm.

The biggest problem with quality circles was scope. Since the groups are made up of workers from a single work area, they cannot address problems that cross organizational boundaries, as many do. By the mid-1980s the media frenzy had turned from how wonderful quality circles were to how they didn't seem to be living up to their promises. Companies that had thousands of operating quality circles in the early 1980s had none by the middle of that decade. By 1987, 80 percent of the Fortune 500 had abandoned quality circles. They were dead, except for the occasional mention in the business press of how quality circles hadn't worked out. America had gotten drunk on the fad, gone to a big quality circle party, and was now waking up with a headache and a management hangover. It certainly didn't want to talk about the embarrassing events of the previous night.

Actually, it isn't quite that simple. Quality circles were often implemented in a faddish way, but by 1992 almost half of American manufacturing companies still had something in place that looked a bit like quality circles. The fad wasn't dead, it had just changed. As Cole asks: "For a movement that had been declared dead for at least a decade and come to be the subject of derision, QCs seem to have shown surprising vitality. How can one recognize this seeming contradiction?"

The reconciliation lies in the fact that quality circles—employee groups solving manufacturing problems—were not really a bad idea; they were simply done badly. The tribal (with bits of wishful) thinking of the time pushed managers to do what everyone else was doing without adapting it to their own situation. Non-manufacturing operations, for instance, are much less appropriate for this type of program than manufacturing concerns, and all implementers needed to make quality programs work with their own people, in their own way. When they didn't do this, the quality circle approach failed; those who did change the program to fit their business eventually—if ten years later than should have been the case—came up with something they could use, although it wasn't quality circles as they initially appeared.

I have probably been a bit hard on American managers in this section. The point is not that they are dummies; they are not. Today the best intellects in the country are in the commercial world, but that's just the point. Smart people do stupid things sometimes, especially when everyone else is doing the same.

Groupthink: The Bay of Pigs

This case is derived from work done by Yale psychologist Irving Janis in the 1970s and 1980s on a phenomenon he called "Groupthink." Janis blamed a number of American policy fiascoes in part on the way small groups of people work together. The quotes in this chapter all all taken from Janis' book, *Groupthink*. These errors fit the category of tribal thinking very well. Janis also applied his model to the escalation of the Vietnam War, America's errors at Pearl Harbor, and the Watergate cover-up, but the Bay of Pigs case is a great example of how small groups of very smart people can get caught up by tribal thought processes and do things they would never have done otherwise.

The Bay of Pigs fiasco actually started in 1954, the year that the government of Jacobo Arbenz Guzmán in Guatemala decided to confiscate for redistribution the assets of a number of American companies. This included assets of the United Fruit Company, now Chiquita. The Guatemalans refused to go before an international court to discuss compensation, and United Fruit began to lobby the U.S. government to take some action in response to the expropriation. United Fruit was well connected in Washington. Among its friends there was Secretary of State John Foster Dulles, who had once been a lawyer for the company. In June 1954 the Central Intelligence Agency (CIA) orchestrated a takeover of Guatemala by Colonel Carlos Castillo Armas. It should be noted that this victory was not obtained by the small force the CIA landed in Guatemala, but by the fact that the Guatemalan army turned on the leftist Arbenz government and removed it. This success led the CIA to believe that intervention in smaller countries was a reasonable and safe activity and paved the way for the debacle at the Bay of Pigs.

In 1959 Fidel Castro overthrew the dictatorship of Fulgencia Batista and took control of Cuba. He also began nationalizing American property and started to exhibit a general leaning toward the Soviet Union.

In 1960 President Eisenhower approved a fairly limited CIA plan to train Cuban exiles and send them back to the island as guerrillas to work for the overthrow of the Castro government, and to support them with a propaganda campaign. The CIA soon developed a more ambitious plan to land a larger number of troops and actually invade the island.

In January 1961 the new president, John Kennedy, and his top advisors were briefed on this new approach and in April approved the plan for execution.

On April 15, 1961, a group of B-26s bombed Cuban airfields, destroying a large part of that nation's air force, and then flew back to land in the United States, where it was announced that the pilots were defecting Cuban patriots. In reality, they were Americans.

On April 17 a group of about 1,400 Cuban exiles landed at the Bay of Pigs, where they were almost immediately cut to pieces by the efficient Cuban military. With no air cover, their supply boats were immediately sunk by the remaining units of the Cuban air force, which then assisted the army in pounding the landing force into submission. Of those troops, 114 were killed and about 1,200 captured; of these 36 eventually died in Cuban prisons.

The political fallout was withering. The United Nations and a number of Latin American countries denounced the United States and the Kennedy administration, the Cuban drift toward the Soviet Union became a sprint, and the Soviets eventually placed nuclear weapons in Cuba. President Kennedy was forced to apologize for the action. He suffered politically at home as well, with large numbers of supporters suddenly becoming cynical about the new administration. Even a hint of the possibility of this kind of political inferno should have convinced the administration to kill the invasion.

Kennedy, crushed by the failure, asked himself: "How could I have been so stupid to let them go ahead?"[17]

One observer wrote that "his anguish was doubly deepened by the knowledge that the rest of the world was asking the same question."

There are actually two levels of failure to discuss pertaining to this incident. First, was it a reasonable plan that failed by accident or unpredictable chance, or simply a stupid plan doomed and unworkable from the beginning? And second, if it was the latter, why didn't anyone see this and stop it?

The answer for the first question is difficult to ferret out. Papers have been published that show that the invasion was simply a bad idea. The Cuban armed forces were too large and too well equipped to be expected to fold instantly. Dictators are well known for keeping the military both happy and well under their control. It was known that the invaders would be outnumbered immediately by an almost ten-to-one margin, with further tens of thousands of Cuban militiamen available to Castro if needed. There was some hope that there would be a spontaneous uprising in support of the invasion by the Cuban people, but the State Department experts who could have shown that this expectation was not realistic were never consulted, due to an ineffective fetish for secrecy around the project.

On the other side of the argument is the fact that for the first day or so the invaders fought well and at least held their own against Castro's army until they ran out of ammunition. The ammunition shortfall was a consequence of the destruction of their supply ships by the Cuban air force, about half of which had survived the initial raids by the B-26s. Their survival was at least partly due to the fact that Kennedy had canceled a second round of bombing raids for fear that they would make American participation too obvious. In this scenario, the root cause of the failure is Kennedy's politically motivated meddling in a military operation.

The government's own investigation into the disaster turned up four important causes for the failure:

1. Failure to subject the project, especially in its latter frenzied stages, to a cold and objective appraisal by the best operating talent available, particularly by those not involved in the operation, such as the chief of operations and the chiefs of the senior staffs. Had this been done, the third and fourth mistakes on this list might have been avoided.

2. Failure to advise the president, at an appropriate time, that success had become dubious and to recommend that the operation be canceled and that the problem of unseating Castro be restudied.

3. Failure to recognize that the project had become overt and that the military effort had become too large to be handled by the agency alone.

4. Failure to reduce successive project plans to formal papers and to leave copies of them with the president and his advisors and to request specific written approval and confirmation of the plans.

Unfortunately, the materials available on the matter are somewhat contradictory and rife with political ax grinding. Some of the problems noted in the report were probably the kind of relatively minor imperfections that plague any operation of this size, and it is difficult to sort through the various opinions to find a definitive answer.

In the end, it is reasonably clear that the Cuban military was simply too big for 1,400 exiles to defeat no matter what else happened, barring the kind of peasant uprising that the CIA knew could not be relied on. Even if this were not the case, it was impossible to be sure that the second set of air attacks would have completely destroyed the Cuban air force. The decision to withhold the second round of air raids was an act of panic, and not very bright, but it was not the reason the operation failed.

Actually, we don't have to determine that the plan was doomed from the start to decide that the policymakers of the Kennedy administration should have known better than to green-light the invasion. There was another operational requirement that was so completely unattainable that it should have stopped the project instantly: the need for secrecy.

It is almost impossible to keep the existence of an operation involving several thousand people secret. Each of those people has family and friends who eventually find out about the action, and they all talk. The newspapers got wind that something was going on and started actively looking for what it might be, and they got to the answer pretty quickly.

While this was happening, Kennedy was assured by his advisors that the plan could be carried out without the world learning that the United States was behind it. For instance, it was assumed that because the B-26s that would carry out the initial bombings would not have U.S. markings, people would believe that they were piloted by defecting Cubans. Apparently no one mentioned that Cuban B-26s all were constructed with a Plexiglas nose, and the planes used in the bombing had the opaque nose of the American version. Anyone could tell the two apart.

Pierre Salinger, Kennedy's press secretary, called the invasion "the least secret covert military operation in history."

Before the invasion, Kennedy himself complained that the operation was compromised in the American newspapers: "I can't believe what I'm reading! Castro doesn't need agents over here. All he has to do is read our papers. It's all laid out for him."

While it may have been possible to maintain "plausible denial" in the broadest diplomatic sense, in which all that is required is a vaguely believable lie to allow adversaries to continue to carry on diplomatic relations, there was no real chance to keep the U.S. role in the invasion secret.

The invasion was doomed from the beginning. The CIA has to bear a large part of the blame for this fiasco, but it is also reasonable to ask where were the men who were supposed to be overseeing the CIA while all this was going on, and why they approved this kind of shaky enterprise.

Given that the invasion was probably not going to topple Castro and that the secrecy Kennedy wanted was not attainable, why did the president and his advisors approve the plan? This is where the Groupthink and tribal thought begins to show up.

Kennedy had a very bright group of advisors. His secretary of state, Dean Rusk, had served in the State Department in the Eisenhower and Truman administrations and had then become head of the Rockefeller

Foundation. He was known as a good administrator with excellent judgment.

Kennedy's secretary of defense, Robert McNamara, had been on the faculty at Harvard (which Kennedy had attended also) and later president of the Ford Motor Company. He was widely regarded as a brilliant individual.

The president's brother, Robert, was attorney general. The appointment of Robert Kennedy, then in his thirties, to this post has been widely criticized as nepotism, which of course it was. But the younger Kennedy was also a bright young man who contributed to his brother's administration.

McGeorge Bundy was Kennedy's Special Assistant for National Security Affairs. He was another Harvard import who had been dean of arts and sciences there and studied the policies of Secretary of State Dean Acheson. Harvard historian Arthur Schlesinger was also part of the team as a special assistant to President Kennedy.

The final two members of the immediate decision-making team were carryovers from the Eisenhower administration, and it was they who conceived and proposed the invasion. Allen Dulles and Richard Bissell were director and deputy director of the CIA, respectively. Both men were respected and quickly accepted into Kennedy's inner circle.

Kennedy and his advisors were clearly an intelligent group. One criticism of the team has been that it was too homogeneous and long on Harvard academics who had spent more time studying the actions of others than doing things themselves. We have seen before how homogeneous groups can get themselves into trouble. Remember that many of the leaders of Long-Term Capital Management had similar backgrounds and beliefs before the company came to grief. A similar situation occurred in the Detroit automakers before they were overrun by the imports in the 1970s. Besides limiting the viewpoints the group can employ on a given problem, homogeneity is also troublesome in that it tends to increase the cohesiveness of the group, the value the members put on the group, and their desire to remain part of it and not violate its rules.

Irving Janis describes several areas where cohesive groups, like Kennedy's advisors, can make predictable mistakes based on the way the group functions:

- Illusion of invulnerability
- Illusion of unanimity and suppression of personal doubts

- Self-appointed mindguards
- Docility fostered by suave leadership
- Taboo against antagonizing valuable new members

Illusion of Invulnerability Cohesive groups seem to have trouble acknowledging that things can go wrong. It may be that group members simply don't want to cast a negative light on any group project, but at any rate, the Kennedy team clearly seemed to suffer from the illusion of invulnerability.

One Justice Department source had this to say:

> It seemed that, with John Kennedy leading us and with all the talent he had assembled, nothing could stop us. We believed that if we faced up to the nation's problems and applied bold, new ideas with common sense and hard work, we would overcome whatever challenged us.

> Schlesinger sounded a similar note about the inner circle: "Everyone around him [Kennedy] thought he had the Midas touch and could not lose. . . . Euphoria reigned; we thought for a moment that the world was plastic and the future unlimited."

This could simply be characterized as wishful thinking, but in this case it is tightly tied to group membership, rather than the less-defined overoptimism that we looked at earlier. This is a fairly natural thing for group members to believe. If you place great value on the group, it makes sense that you would be very confident that the group will generally be successful, and things will work out right for its members. This showed up in the Bay of Pigs case in the assumption of Kennedy's team that the whole world would accept their lame story about how the United States was not involved in the invasion despite clear proof otherwise.

Illusion of Unanimity and Suppression of Personal Doubts People like to have their groups free of discord. A group that is unanimous in a belief indicates that the belief must be correct; otherwise certainly someone would have seen the flaw in it. Disagreements are dangerous; they can destroy the group, or at least force some members out of it. We will address these two of Janis's Groupthink elements together since they stem from the same source, the desire not to oppose the rest of the group. Here is what Schlesinger said about his own failure to speak up against the invasion plan:

> In the months after the Bay of Pigs I bitterly reproached myself for having kept so silent during those crucial discussions in the Cabinet Room, though my feelings of guilt were tempered by the knowledge that a course of objection would have accomplished little save to gain me a name as a nuisance. I can only explain my failure to do more than raise a few timid questions by reporting that one's impulse to blow the whistle on this nonsense was simply undone by the circumstances of the discussion.

In other words, Schlesinger didn't say anything because he didn't think anyone would listen. This is natural enough, if not the kind of leadership one expects from the best and brightest in a nation of then 200 million people.

This reluctance to voice objections has the effect of preventing discussion, and apparently the discussion of the invasion was extremely limited. Kennedy and his advisors, it turns out, had very different ideas about just what the operation would be, indicating that no substantial discussion took place.

There is one place in which Schlesinger might have been wrong in his assessment, and that is in the idea that any objection would have been futile. He himself says in another instance: "Had one senior advisor opposed the adventure, I believe that Kennedy would have cancelled it. No one spoke against it."

Not always, but sometimes it only takes a single voice to turn the tide. Granted, that voice has to speak with some authority and passion, but one rational thought sometimes can bring the group to its senses. Then again, perhaps nothing would have changed. Senator William Fulbright, a respected voice from the Democratic party, had spoken to Kennedy's team, telling the group that this invasion was wrong-headed and immoral, and his words had no effect. But Fulbright was an outsider, and his voice did not carry the weight that a senior advisor's would have.

Self-Appointed Mindguards   "Mindguard" is Irving Janis's term for group members who put pressure on those who are deviating from group norms to bring them back into the fold and keep them from disrupting the nice, consensual atmosphere. When Schlesinger's objections became known to Robert Kennedy, he took the historian aside and said to him: "You may be right or you may be wrong, but the President has made his mind up. Don't push it any further. Now is the time for everyone to help him all they can."

Dean Rusk also apparently operated in a Mindguard role by preventing Undersecretary of State Chester Bowles from making his objections to the plan known to the president's senior team.

Docility Fostered by Suave Leadership   This is Janis's term for a variety of leadership practices that can suppress dissent. They include such practices as controlling who talks at meetings and how much time is spent on various topics. There is some evidence that Kennedy fell into this trap. For instance, when Bowles attended a group meeting in place of Rusk and was "horrified" at the ease with which the group was accepting the CIA plan, Kennedy did not provide the opportunity for the group to hear from a fresh mind on the topic by allowing Bowles to speak. The practice of keeping potential dissenters silent stems from the same desire to maintain group consensus as other Mindguarding practices.

Taboo against Antagonizing Valuable New Members   Dulles and Bissell, while holdovers from the Eisenhower administration, were well regarded and accepted by Kennedy's team. Bissell especially was recognized as an organized, articulate, and intelligent team member. It may be that the special standing of these men—team members who were recently outsiders—led the team to defer to them. It is commonly recognized that when groups are first formed, they go through a period where the members feel each other out and form relationships. During this period members typically are polite and refrain from argument. Bissell and Dulles probably benefited a bit from a deference given to new members to avoid offending them before they are totally integrated into the group, and this may be why they were not challenged with more vigor on their plan.

Taken as a whole, the evidence is fairly conclusive that Kennedy and his top advisors never gave the Bay of Pigs invasion plan the kind of attention and debate it deserved and that the reasons for this were rooted in the cozy group atmosphere of the team. This lack of healthy dissent can happen in any group, and good leaders know how to prevent it. It may be significant that Kennedy's team, while very bright, was made up of people with limited leadership experience. With the exception of McNamara, they did not have a great deal of background managing this kind of effort, and that lack of experience may have been what made them vulnerable.

■ NOTES

1. S. E. Asch, "Effects of Group Pressure upon the Modification and Distortion of Judgements," in *Groups, Leadership and Men*, ed. H. Guetzkow (Pittsburgh, PA: Carnegie Press, 1951): 177–190 and S. E. Asch, "Studies of Independence and Submission to Group Pressure: I. A Minority of One against a Unanimous Majority," *Psychological Monograph* 70, no. 9 (1956).
2. S. Moscovici and C. Faucheux, "Social Influence, Conforming Bias, and the Study of Active Minorities," in *Advances in Experimental Social Psychology*, ed. L. Berkowitz (New York: Academic Press, 1972): pp. 149-2-2.
3. J. A. F. Stoner, "A Comparison of Individual and Group Decision Involving Risk" (master's thesis, Massachusetts Institute of Technology, 1961).
4. Donna Kossey, *Strange Creations: Aberrant Ideas of Human Origins from Ancient Astronauts to Aquatic Apes* (Los Angeles: Feral House, 2001).
5. Ibid.
6. Ben Klassen, *Nature's Eternal Religion* (World Church of the Creator, 1973).
7. George James, *Stolen Legacy: Greek Philosophy Is Stolen Egyptian Philosophy* (New York, Africa World Press, 1954).
8. Frances Cress Welsing, *The Isis Papers: The Keys to the Colors* (Chicago: Third World Press, 1991).
9. Ibid.
10. Tom Davenport, "Interview: Peter F. Drucker—A Meeting of the Minds," *CIO Magazine*, September 15, 1997.
11. John Micklethwait and Adrian Wooldrige, *The Witch Doctors* (New York: Times Books, 1996).
12. Lucy Kellaway, "Volumes in Learning—Take It as Read," *Financial Times* (London), September 12, 1995.
13. John Micklethwait and Adrian Wooldrige, *The Witch Doctors* (New York: Times Books, 1996).
14. Robert E. Cole, *Managing Quality Fads: How American Business Learned to Play the Quality Game* (New York: Oxford University Press, 1999).
15. Tom Davenport, "Interview: Peter F. Drucker—A Meeting of the Minds," *CIO Magazine*, September 15, 1997.
16. Robert E. Cole, *Managing Quality Fads: How American Business Learned to Play the Quality Game* (New York: Oxford University Press, 1999).
17. Irving L. Janis, *Groupthink* (Boston: Houghton Mifflin, 1982).

Royal Thinking

There are two elements to royal thinking: overconfidence and hierarchy. The rationale for placing these two sets of problems together is simply that in my experience, they both are often associated with authority. People in authority are smart and successful; they have had the kind of positive feedback about their decision-making abilities that makes people confident. They also preside over hierarchies of subordinates, which creates its own decision-making problems, often magnifying the problems created by overconfidence.

In some ways, authority of the kind we have today is unnatural. In a tribe of apes there is a pecking order, some individuals having higher status than others, but you don't really find authority, just an agreement about who has first access to food and sex. However, although we did not evolve with authority as it exists today, we did evolve with a dominance hierarchy, and we are wired to respect that. This is the root of royal thinking. Any animal group that is at all social employs some kind of dominance hierarchy. Apes can have fairly complex hierarchical relationships, and even chickens have their "pecking order." These straightforward hierarchies work fairly well in the wild (actually, by civilized standards, they work abominably, but they do keep the tribe alive and breeding) but not as well in the modern world, where the role of brute, immediate power is diluted, hierarchies are large, and tasks are more complex.

Primitive societies may have authority structures, but they are confined to small groups, since these preagricultural societies can't produce enough food to support large numbers of people. Also, in a hunter-gatherer tribe, the tasks undertaken by the group are fairly simple, moving from place to place or hunting a large animal. One person can have all the knowledge necessary to accomplish the task and doesn't need to supervise in areas he or she isn't familiar with. With agriculture and the beginning of civilization, there came a time when there was enough surplus food so that large amounts of manpower were available for other tasks. This allowed the rise of the "local strongman," someone with the resources to do things like build pyramids for the glorification of himself and his ancestors. At this point the standard hierarchy of authority we know today came into existence. One person supervises a group, and that person reports to someone higher up the chain, until you get to the ultimate authority: the king. There are also the gods, of course, who decreed that the king should rule everybody else, at least as long as he gave a good cut of the loot to the priests and didn't horn in on the temple revenues.

This model (leaving out the gods) is a lot like what we have in place today in almost every aspect of life. Privates report to corporals, who report to sergeants; laborers report to foremen, who report to supervisors; bureaucrats report to other bureaucrats with greater power; priests report to bishops; and so on.

There are one or two other models out there. For instance, a small number of businesses use "self-managed teams," where there is not really a supervisor, but in general the hierarchical model of authority has been unchanged for thousands of years and essentially rules the world.

The assumption underlying this model is that individual workers know their jobs and are the people most familiar with what is needed to accomplish it, and that supervisors know a bit less about the job but have a broader perspective on the goals of the organization and how various jobs interrelate. Supervisors are generally more senior and may have proven themselves as individual contributors earlier in their careers. However, this model opens the group up for some predictable mistakes:

- **Simple overconfidence.** Most of us are a bit overconfident in our own judgment. Supervisors have been rewarded with command, perhaps for good performance, perhaps simply for good politicking; this can leave them dangerously overconfident in their own decision-making abilities and resistant to ideas other than their own. In addition, the effect of hierarchy can magnify this tendency in several other ways that will be described later.

- **Misplaced confidence.** Closely related to simple overconfidence, misplaced confidence describes those situations where thinkers are used to operating in an area where they have great expertise and carry their confidence from those areas over into unrelated pursuits where their skills are small or nonexistent. Hierarchy can make this worse because managerial distance, the next mistake, forces supervisors to manage areas in which they are not expert.

- **Managerial distance.** Supervisors or managers often have authority over things with which they are only vaguely familiar, especially as they are promoted several times. It can be very difficult for managers to know when to overrule a subordinate who is more knowledgeable about the specific issue at hand, but not familiar with broader elements of the problem. At the same time it can be difficult not to overrule a subordinate whose expertise counsels an approach that will not meet the organization's immediate goals but may still be correct in the long term. In the *Challenger* shuttle disaster to be discussed, we will see how managers can be tempted to overrule a more knowledgeable subordinate to meet a short-term management goal. In general, these problems can be characterized in one of two ways: overmanagement, in which the person in authority inserts himself too much into the way things are done, or undermanagement, where the person in authority is not involved enough in day-to-day work.

- **Cronyism.** Being tasked with achieving a result and having no idea how to go about it places managers in very difficult positions. For this reason some leaders begin to rely on subordinates who project an aura of confidence, do not challenge the leaders' opinions, and generally tell the leaders what they want to hear. Leaders can end up transferring the unwarranted confidence they might otherwise have had in themselves to this crony. Powerful leaders at the end of their careers seem especially vulnerable to doing this. For instance, as he entered his dotage, Henry Ford gave great latitude to Harry Bennett, to the lasting detriment of his company. Cronyism is not restricted to old men, however, nor is it always this obvious.

- **Managing up and managing appearances to improve status.** Because leaders are expected to be right and to be in charge, it is difficult for some leaders to admit mistakes. This is especially true if the admission must be made upward in the chain of command. Many people spend so much time managing their boss that they don't manage their work and are so concerned with appearance and status that they fail to give proper weight to other issues.

- **Silence of subordinates.** Because leaders have power over subordinates, sometimes a subordinate hesitates or refuses to contradict the leader, even when it is obvious that the leader is wrong. This can further strengthen the leader's unwarranted confidence. We saw this with the little girls in the Conan Doyle case in Chapter 2 who couldn't tell such important people they were wrong.

- **Elimination of talent.** Finally, leaders become so overbearing that other talented people will not work with them.

Royal thinking is the root cause of some cases where no single individual seems to have made a mistake. Everyone acted correctly based on the information available to them. However, people at the top made the decision without the information and counsel of the people at the bottom, and afterward they were seen slapping their foreheads and lamenting that they would have made the right call "if I had only known." They would have known had they not been so confident (simple overconfidence) and so insulated from the people closest to the work (managerial distance).

My favorite example of the corrupting effects of power on thought occurred in 1893. Admiral Sir George Tyron of the British Royal Navy was in command of a group of ships traveling in two parallel lines. The admiral, who wanted to turn his ships around to head in the opposite direction, mistakenly ordered that both lines turn inward, toward the other, to turn around.

Geometry is a merciless science. The combined turning radius of the battleships HMS *Victoria* and HMS *Camperdown* was less than the distance between the lines of ships. The *Camperdown* rammed the *Victoria*, which sank, killing many of the men aboard, including the admiral. Some of the other officers on board had seen what was going to happen, but the admiral had not thought to check with anyone else, and his subordinates had feared to question his directive. This is royal thinking of the overconfidence and the silence-of-subordinate types.

These problems can surface not just in formal, structured hierarchies, but also around informal leadership provided by supposed experts. One of the dangers of expertise is that the expert doesn't always know where her knowledge ends. Again, this is illustrated powerfully in the case of Henry Ford. Ford was a mechanical genius, but ignorant about many other things. When he got a hunch about an engine, the result could be, and was in one case, the first low-cost V8 engine designed for mass production. When he got a hunch about something else, the result could be hopelessly ridiculous, like the time he loaded a ship with peace activists and thought that by sailing to Europe, he could stop World War I. Later he almost bankrupted his company by refusing to adopt a number of business practices, such as offering credit and updating his successful but outdated Model T. Ford was not disposed to take the advice of anyone else, including his own son, on most subjects, and again, some of his advisors manipulated him for their own advancement.

Leadership is about being decisive. Most people will remember the movie *Apollo 13* staring Tom Hanks as Jim Lovell and Ed Harris as Gene Kranz. When an explosion takes place on the space capsule, Kranz takes charge of the situation on the ground, telling his staff: "Work the problem; let's not make it worse by guessing."

At that point the chaos at mission control evaporates as the staff members turn to their procedures to begin searching for solutions. Eventually Kranz makes the decision to take the spacecraft around the moon rather than try to turn it around and head straight back to Earth. I had occasion to hear Gene Kranz speak a few years ago and was, by blind chance, fortunate enough to sit with him at lunch. In discussing the movie and the events it portrayed, he commented that "one of the functions of leadership is to shield your people from uncertainty," meaning that, in a situation like the one portrayed in the film, someone has to make a decision about the direction to take and get everyone moving rather than leave them paralyzed by uncertainty. This is one of the functions of leadership in the real world, but it is also one of the reasons that leaders sometimes err on the side of trusting their own opinions too much. There are not many *Apollo 13* situations in everyday life, but the tendency to take one's own intuition as gospel can become very strong after years of success. It is easy to just make a decision.

But most leaders can find times during their careers when they said to themselves "Why on earth didn't I ask anyone about that? Anybody could have told me it was a mistake." It is a fairly common error born of the need to be in charge. If you ask everyone else about everything you do, you aren't leading.

SCIENCE

Many of us tend toward overconfidence in our own abilities. This has been shown fairly clearly in the laboratory. When you look at a range of studies of how overconfident people are, one fact jumps out. People are less overconfident in areas that they know a lot about and more overconfident in areas about which they are ignorant. Apparently if we don't know a lot about something, we figure that it must be fairly simple. A famous experiment supports the idea that hierarchy can have negative effects on cognition.[1] The subjects would come into a room with the experimenter and another subject. The experiment was explained as a test of learning. One person (the learner) would be asked to memorize pairs of words; the other (the teacher) would administer an electric shock to the learner whenever he got one of the pairs wrong. Each shock would be a little more powerful than the last, going up in 15-volt increments to a maximum of 450 volts. As the shocks become stronger, the learner starts to feel real discomfort and then pain, eventually begging that the shocks be stopped. The experimenter ignores the learner's cries of pain and directs the teacher to administer the next shock. In fact, the learner is just acting, he isn't being shocked at all, and the purpose of the experiment is to see how far the real subject—the teacher—will go.

The amazing thing about this experiment was that not one of the forty subjects stopped administering shocks before 300 volts, when the learner was screaming in pain; in fact, about two thirds went all the way to 450 volts. This experiment was so shocking (sorry) that it has been replicated over and over by puzzled researchers seeking to find out what was going on and perhaps invalidate these findings. It has been repeated with men, women, people of different ages, subjects who cry out that they have heart trouble, and every other permutation researchers have been able to think of, and the results hold up. The people administering the shocks are not sadists; they ask the experimenter to stop, sometimes beg to stop, and are eventually reduced to twitching wrecks, but they keep throwing the switches.

This experiment is the best possible evidence for the ability of authority to make us do things we would not normally do. The authority of the person running the experiment, the "man in charge," is the reason people keep pulling those switches. If an authority figure you never saw before today can make two thirds of us do this, imagine what a more powerful figure can do to our thoughts. The result of this wiring is the silence-of-subordinates type of royal thinking.

CASES

Margaret Peter

In the modern world, cults provide extreme examples of both tribal and royal thinking. The cult leader typically has complete control over his or her followers and can make them do almost anything, including take their own lives, as Jim Jones did to his followers. A smaller, less complicated version of the effects of cult leadership can be found in the case of Margaret Peter.

Margaret Peter was a charismatic woman and religious leader who, in 1823 in a small German town, provided us with a wonderful and horrible example of royal thinking. Margaret was a precocious child and had become something of an in-family religious guru to her sisters and father by the time she was a teen. She did a spell as an itinerant preacher and returned home to live with, and rule, her family and continue to preach the word of God as she heard it. Like a lot of cult leaders, Margaret seemed interested in end-of-the-world lore and in the presence of Satan in the everyday world.

One day she announced to her flock, which consisted of her sisters, their husbands, and some hired servants, that Satan was living in the family's attic, whereupon the group demolished the offending room with hammers and clubs.

Margaret then told the group that she had to be crucified, but was interrupted when her sister Elizabeth offered herself as a replacement and hit herself on the head with a hammer to show that she was ready to die. With Margaret's assurance that Elizabeth would be resurrected, the flock immediately beat the young woman to death with the instruments they happened to still have at hand from demolishing the attic.

Unfortunately, this was not enough. Margaret told the flock that she still had to be crucified, cracking herself on the head with a hammer, as Elizabeth had done, for emphasis. So her loyal followers pried up a few floorboards and nailed her to them. Crucifixion does not kill the victim right away, which is one of the reasons the Romans employed it so enthusiastically, and a member of the flock had to shatter Margaret's skull with a crowbar to get the process moving. But since Margaret had promised that she would be gone only for a bit, the group decided to just get on with things and not hold dinner for her.

Three days later the only life in the bodies of Elizabeth and Margaret Peters was a cloud of flies, and the prayers of the faithful continued to go unanswered.

Cult leaders like Margaret Peters are simply extreme examples of leaders becoming crazed by the unquestioning belief of their followers and losing touch with the reality of the everyday world. In these cases, the natural human tendency toward overconfidence is swollen until leaders imagine that there is nothing that they cannot do, including rising from the dead in this case. Elizabeth also demonstrates the kind of blind faith in a leader that characterizes the silence-of-subordinates error type, although in this case it manifested in aggressive, rather than passive, support. We will see less extreme examples in some of the cases that follow.

Nick Leeson and Barings Bank

In everyday life the most common type of royal thought is a combination of overconfidence and managerial distance. Managerial distance is the tendency of people at the top of a hierarchy to get out of touch with what is going on below them. The king is above it all and doesn't have to understand the work of the kingdom; there are servants for that, after all. In the Barings Bank case we see the effects of overconfidence, combined with the disjunction of leadership from reality. The leaders of Barings Bank were so far removed from the goings-on in their business that a twenty-eight-year-old clerk/trader was able to destroy their enterprise through their own undermanagement.

In 1995 Barings was the oldest bank in England. Originally founded as a cloth and wool trading partnership in 1762, it had a storied history. It had helped to fund the Napoleonic wars, and by 1818 the Duc de Richelieu would say that "there are six great powers in Europe: England, France, Prussia, Austria, Russia and Baring Brothers."[2]

While Barings was not an especially large bank in 1995, particularly in comparison to some of the great American and Japanese banks of the time, it was solid and well respected.

Nick Leeson, the man who was to bring down Barings, had humbler roots. He was born in 1969 in Watford, Hertfordshire, England. His father was a plasterer, his mother a nurse. He is remembered by classmates as a "regular guy" who gave no indications that he would someday destroy a 250-year-old pillar of finance. After leaving school he went to work for Coutts & Co., a London bank, as a clerk, and then went to Morgan Stanley as a clerk settling futures and options trades. Again, his contemporaries there do not remember him as remarkable.

Any trading operation, such as Leeson worked in at Morgan Stanley and later at Barings, can be broadly divided into two parts. There is the "front-office" business of standing in a trading pit and actually doing the trade, which is performed by highly compensated traders and often driven by intense and sophisticated research, and there is the "back-office" task of settling up the trade afterward. "Settlement" means making sure that if your person in the pit traded 2,000 shares of a company to someone else, you log the trade into the computer, see that the shares change hands, and get the various currencies used to match up, among other things.

Leeson joined the Barings settlements department in 1989, and to all accounts was fairly good at his job. His first big success came in 1990, when he was asked to lead a team charged with sorting out a huge back-office mess in the company's Jakarta, Indonesia, office. Barings had executed a number of trades for stocks and had accepted the wrong stock certificates in settling them. When the stock market had fallen, many clients who had bought stock through Barings had refused to accept delivery of the certificates because of poor documentation and incorrect serial numbers on the certificates. Leeson and his team slogged through these trades one at a time, eventually setting right about £100 million in trades.

Leeson spent much of 1990 and 1991 doing special projects, often related to financial derivatives. A derivative is a financial instrument whose value is based on an underlying asset. The two most straightforward types of derivatives are futures and options.

A futures contract is an agreement between a buyer and seller for the seller to deliver, and the buyer to accept, a particular amount of something (like a stock) at a future time for an agreed-on price. An option is a contract that gives the holder the right to buy or sell at a specified price during a specified time period. Unlike a futures contract, an option does not require that the holder of the option take any action; it is the holder's "option" whether to do so or not. Derivative trading can be extremely complex, and very few people at Barings really understood it. Leeson said in his autobiography:

> . . . returned to London in March 1991, and from then on was seen as the settlements expert in futures and options. . . . People at the London end of Barings were all so know-all that nobody dared ask a stupid question in case they looked silly in front of everyone else. I always found that the most basic, obvious questions are the ones which are most difficult to answer, and which normally bring out the crucial piece of missing knowledge.[3]

In this statement Leeson captured at least one of the problems that resulted in Barings allowing him to make unauthorized trades for two years and destroy the firm. The practice of managing appearances so as to not appear uninformed frequently contributes to complex mistakes. The other aspect of this case is the issue of management distance. Leeson's superiors had no idea what he was doing even when he appeared to be contributing an unrealistically large portion of the firm's profit. There was also a bit of misplaced confidence here in that Leeson's superiors probably felt that they could manage him even though they knew nothing about what he was doing.

In 1992 Leeson was assigned to set up and run both the front- and back-office operations for Barings' new trading function in Singapore, on the Singapore International Monetary Exchange (SIMEX). A couple of problems are immediately apparent in this decision. Leeson had no experience as a trader and little background in executing trades. Also, it is widely understood in trading circles that it is a dangerous practice to have the same person in charge of both front- and back-office operations. Despite the higher status and greater compensation of the front-office jobs, the back office has an oversight role in keeping the front office honest. If a trader makes a mistake—for instance, buys when she was supposed to have sold—she can't hide it because she has no access to the settlement process that is performed by the back office. Having the same person in charge of both functions is viewed rather like asking the fox to guard the henhouse. Yet this was exactly what Barings' management did in placing Leeson in this position. To make matters worse, Leeson did not have an effective chain of command. This lack of a clear management structure reflected tension between the

London office and the branch offices such as Singapore. In a prescient memo, James Bax, the head of Barings' Singapore office said:

> My concern is that we are once again in danger of setting up a structure that will subsequently prove disastrous and with which we will succeed in losing either a lot of money or client good will or probably both. . . . In my view it is critical that we should keep clear reporting lines, and if this office is involved in SIMEX, then Nick should report to Simon [Jones, the Operations Manager for Southeast Asia] and then be ultimately responsible for the operations side.[4]

As it turned out, Leeson didn't really have a boss. Simon Jones seemed to supervise some aspects of his operation. Mike Killian, who ran a trading operation in Tokyo, also had some supervisory duties and Ron Baker, who was in charge of Global Financial Products, was probably the closest thing Leeson had to a boss. Killian knew about derivative markets, but he was the farthest removed from Leeson's day-to-day operations. Baker, who should have been closest to Leeson, had little knowledge of derivatives. This is where the issue of management distance creeps in. With no boss, to whom was Leeson accountable?

It is not entirely clear why Leeson began making unauthorized trades. In his autobiography, he claims that he started doing it to hide mistakes made by his staff. When a trader in the front office would perform the wrong trade or make some other error, Leeson would, in his role as head of the back office, bury the mistake in a special error account, which is precisely the reason you shouldn't have one person in charge of both functions. Leeson claims that the reason for the errors was that one of his bosses, Mike Killian, refused to allow him to pay salaries high enough to attract good people. A more sinister explanation is that he intended to trade using the firm's money, unknown to his superiors, and planned to take the profits for himself.

There is no way to know for certain which of these explanations is most nearly correct. I lean toward one that is in between, but closer to Leeson's than to some of his critics. Put yourself in his position. You don't really know how to run a front-office operation, and when your staff starts making mistakes, you don't know how to prevent them in the future, except perhaps to fire the person involved, which is an unpleasant solution and won't fix a problem that is part of the process itself. A big error happens. You have been working hard and making money for the firm, but this wipes out all your good efforts, all because someone heard an order wrong. You, a working-class boy, are on the verge of a six-figure bonus, of being a real player in the market, but now you are going to be fired and probably will never get another chance like this again. So you hide the error, not knowing what else to do. Over the next few days the market moves and the bad trade gets worse. (You still own whatever was bought by mistake, and its value can go up or down; in this case it goes down.) You do this over and over again in the next few months; whenever someone makes a bad mistake, you put it into the error account and hide it. Finally the account is so large and the subterfuge has been going on so long that you won't just be fired, but people will start to ask whether your actions were criminal. Because these mistakes have lost the company money, you start to make unauthorized trades using the firm's money in the hopes of making enough to set things right, while vowing that if you do you will never get in this position again. But your trades go bad, and with each one you lose more and more money.

This is how the situation may have played out with young Mr. Leeson. He certainly began making more and more illicit trades, and the market certainly moved against him. He resorted to all kinds of subterfuge to hide his huge losses, at one point forging a document (by cutting a signature block off of one letter and copying it onto another; apparently even today you just can't beat the old favorites), authenticating a large trade that never took place to hide his activity. Leeson was audited by Barings several times, especially when his success began to look suspicious and members of the media began to notice the huge positions he was taking, but the audits were inept and he was always able to convince the auditors that everything was all right. One audit found that:

> While the individual controls over BFS's [Baring Futures Singapore] system and operations are satisfactory, there is a significant general risk that the controls could be over-ridden by the General Manager [Leeson]. He is the key manager in the front and back office and can thus initiate transactions on the Group's behalf and then ensure that they are settled and recorded according to his own instructions.[5]

The audit suggested that another manager should be inserted to run the back office, and listed a number of tasks that Leeson should quit doing, including such things as signing checks and signing off of reconciliation activities at SIMEX. However, it also said that the company should see that

"BFS's General Manager [Leeson], who makes the key trading decisions, is retained as long as possible. Although there is some strength in depth in the trading team, the loss of his services to a competitor would speed the erosion of BFS's profitability greatly."[6]

Barings' management chose to take no action in response to this and several other audits. Again, this is the issue of management distance. Leeson's superiors simply did not want to be bothered learning what was going on in an operation that was making them money.

While all this was happening, Leeson was developing a reputation as a superstar. His losses were hidden and he was making huge profits for Barings. Baker brought him to London to introduce him to Peter Norris, the CEO of Barings Investment Bank. Just before his house of cards fell apart, Leeson was in line to receive a bonus of £450,000, around $700,000, for his great performance.

But this success also raised eyebrows. Mike Killian said that he remembers thinking: "He was making $10 million in one week—doing arbitrage at SIMEX? And Salomons and CRT have got all the computers and years of experience and he's sucking that much out. That sounds like turbo arbitrage to me. How's he doing this? Christ! Let's shut the rest of the place down."[7]

But this kind of questioning was not enough to get Barings' management to undertake a truly thorough audit of Leeson's activities. He continued to be the organization's superstar, and nobody wanted to look too closely at what he was doing, probably not out of any nefarious desire to hide something, but just from an "it's working, don't fiddle with it" mind-set.

However, there is simply no way to keep losses like Leeson was running up secret forever. On February 23, 1995, with his actions finally about to come to light, Leeson ran, taking his wife and fleeing first to Kuala Lumpur and later to Europe. The next day his superiors received a fax that read:

> My sincere apologies for the predicament that I have left you in. It was neither my intent or aim for this to happen, but the pressures, both business and personal, have become too much to bear and after receiving medical advice, have affected my health to the extent that a breakdown is imminent. In light of my actions I tender my resignation with immediate effect and will contact you early next week to discuss the best course of action. Apologies, Nick.[8]

Leeson had run up almost \$1 billion in debt, an amount Barings could not hope to make good. The twenty-eight-year-old trader had destroyed the 250-year-old bank. Nick Leeson was arrested and went to prison. The remains of the bank were bought by the Dutch firm ING and became part of ING Barings. But can this kind of thing really be blamed on a young clerk? Where were the financial graybeards of the firm while all this was going on?

The failings in Leeson's thought processes are fairly obvious, and not necessarily irrational, except for a healthy dose of wishful thinking that kept him in the market, hoping that it would eventually flip his way. Basically he made mistakes and felt he had no option but to cover them up. But what about his superiors? No one in their right mind gives anyone, let alone a twenty-eight-year-old clerk, the authority to spend hundreds of millions of dollars on his own signature, not when a mistake will destroy the company and the livelihood of all its employees. Yet this is just what was done. London's *Daily Telegraph* suggested this:

> It defies the comprehension of an outsider that a single individual could have wreaked such havoc for almost three years without detection. Mr. Leeson is neither a victim nor a hero, merely the latest in a long history of young men entrusted with responsibilities for which they proved unfit. But it is those who sat on the board of Barings who emerge from this story as almost sublime incompetents, blithely counting their own booty on the promenade deck, oblivious to the torrent cascading into their ship below the waterline.[9]

And it is here that the story becomes interesting for us. Leeson's supervisors were not stupid; they were smart people, although, as is common in finance, not as smart as they were rich. Yet they did some truly stupid things. Among their sins were:

- The initial failure of posting Leeson to the job of running the trading operation, something at which he had no experience.
- Failure to separate Leeson's front-office and back-office functions, despite the fact that this was standard industry practice and despite its being called out as a problem by an auditor.
- Failure to do elementary oversight by matching the cash sent to Leeson to fund his trades with actual client accounts.

- Failure to understand the business that Leeson was in even though it accounted for a significant fraction of the bank's profits.

- Failure to follow up on numerous irregularities in Leeson's business, not least of which was the sheer profitability, but which also included notice from external auditors about documentation irregularities and notice from SIMEX about irregularities in a special error account.

Ron Baker made this comment regarding the issue of lack of management knowledge of the derivative business:

> There is no doubt in my mind that my lack of experience in the area was a contributing factor to what has happened here. All I can say in defense of that is that lack of experience is something that I have overcome before in my life when I have taken things on, but if you ally lack of experience to the lack of information I got and to the other failures in the organization, in the failure to give me accurate information . . . then I think that meant getting up a learning curve which was impossible. There is no doubt in my mind that if I had had ten years experience in exchange-traded equity derivatives, this would not have happened. The fact is, I did not.[10]

In Baker's mind, the problem was not that he didn't understand his own business, but the combination of that lack of understanding with the other aspects of the case. In his mind, it should have been okay for him to be ignorant about his business, if only everything else had been right. I would suggest that a real pro of a manager would not have allowed this situation to continue. If he did not understand a business of this magnitude, he would have found someone who did and brought that person in as an advisor. Certainly more than one person in an organization must understand a business that is so central to its profitability, and if Leeson was simply a solo superstar, as Baker thought at the time, why wasn't someone making a detailed study of his methods to employ them elsewhere?

We also see in Baker's statement something that defines royal thinking. He has had success before; thus he is overconfident. Combine this with the wishful thinking engendered by the fact that Nick Leeson was helping make Ron Baker a huge bonus, and the general insulation of management and the resulting undermanagement, and you have the recipe for a great disaster.

Challenger Disaster

The *Challenger* disaster shows yet another aspect of royal thinking: the tendency for leaders who are far removed from the front-line knowledge that is necessary to make good decisions to go ahead and make them anyway. It also shows the negative impact of the politics of status in-group decision making, which was the reason that the key issues in the *Challenger* crash were not brought to the attention of higher authorities within NASA.

The launch of the space shuttle *Challenger* was an important and highly visible occasion for NASA. It marked the first time that a civilian, teacher Christa McAuliffe, would journey into space and the launch would be observed in person by the vice president of the United States, an important advocate for NASA.

The launch was dogged by bad luck from the start. It was delayed five times—a NASA record—due to bad weather and mechanical difficulties. When it finally launched on the morning of January 28, 1986, the rocket survived only 73 seconds before exploding, killing all seven crew members and becoming one of America's most painful national tragedies.

Why did it happen? There are two answers, one addressing the physical processes that led to the disaster and another telling the tale of how those physical processes, which we understand fairly well, were allowed to occur. Let's start with the accident itself.

The space shuttle looks something like a school bus might if it had to fly; it is short and thick, with small wings. At launch the shuttle is attached to a large external tank, much larger than the shuttle itself, which holds hydrogen and oxygen for fuel. On each side of the external tank are the two cylindrical solid rocket boosters (SRBs). Each of these is 149 feet long and 12 feet in diameter. The SRBs burn during takeoff to help the shuttle blast its way out of Earth's gravity and are then jettisoned, retrieved, and reused. Because the SRBs are too long to transport conveniently, they are shipped in seven cylindrical sections, which are then hooked together at the launch site to form the complete 149-foot-long rocket. The joint between these sections is what is called a tang-and-clevis arrangement and is referred to as a field joint, since it is installed in the field rather than at the factory. The wall of the lower section of the rocket is shaped like a ∪; this is the clevis. The tang, on the upper section, is a straight spine of metal that goes inside the ∪ of the clevis, thus keeping the two sections from sliding across each other. A large number of pins then hold the joint together.

January 28 was clear but cold in Florida. The temperature was 36 degrees Fahrenheit (F), 15 degrees colder than any other shuttle launch. At 11:38 ~AM Eastern Standard Time the space shuttle *Challenger* lifted off its pad at the Kennedy Space Center. Videotape of the launch shows that at 0.68 seconds after launch there is black smoke coming from the aft (bottom) field joint of the right SRB. The smoke stopped 2.7 seconds into the launch but was an indication that the joint was not sealing correctly. Combustion residue from the burning fuel temporarily sealed the faulty joint, but at about 58 seconds into the flight the *Challenger* ran into a violent wind shear, which shook the residue loose and allowed the combustion gases to escape again. At 58.8 seconds into the flight a small flame can be seen coming from the joint. This flame eventually burned through a strut attaching the SRB to the external tank and then through the external tank itself. The flame initially burned into the section of the tank containing hydrogen, but the violent action of the escaping hydrogen, combined with the now barely restrained SRB banging into the external tank, also ruptured the oxygen tank. Hydrogen and oxygen together are an explosive combination, which of course is why they can fuel a rocket. At just over 73 seconds of flight the *Challenger* was engulfed in a ball of flame and disintegrated while traveling just under twice the speed of sound. The astronauts were probably not killed by the explosion; even if they were not, the sudden loss of cabin pressure probably rendered them unconscious until they were killed when the crew module struck the water minutes later after a 50,000-foot fall.

What caused the SRB joint to leak the superheated gas that destroyed the *Challenger*? To understand this we must look more closely at the design of the rocket.

To prevent the hot gas from inside the rocket from escaping through the tang and clevis joint, a strip of rubber is fitted into grooves on the inside leg of the clevis. There it can press up against both the tang and clevis, thus sealing the gases inside. Because this rubber seal has to go all the way around the rocket, it is in the shape of a ring and is called an "O-ring." An O-ring is a fairly common way to seal anything in the shape of a tube or cylinder—a pipe joint, for instance—and was used successfully on the Titan booster rocket, the SRB's predecessor. To be doubly safe, two O-rings were used, one above the other. To protect the rubber O-rings from the hot rocket gases, a heat-resistant putty was put over them so that, ideally, the gases would never actually touch the O-rings. The pressure of the propulsion gases was used to press the O-rings into place and make a good seal. Thus, it took a few milliseconds, depending on atmospheric temperature, as we shall see, for the O-rings to seal properly.

There were some known problems with these field joints, and the maker of the SRB, Morton-Thiokol, was working on a new design to eliminate them. For one thing, when the rockets fired, the intense pressure of the propulsion gases caused the walls of the rocket to balloon outward. This deformation made it possible for a gap to open in the tang and clevis arrangement. Thiokol had made some changes to minimize this, but the issue was not completely resolved. In addition, the O-rings were often eaten away during launch. In some cases there was soot and grease on the outside of the rocket, indicating that some of the rocket gases were actually blowing past the O-rings and escaping. In investigating this issue, Thiokol looked at different types of heat-resistant putty and investigated the behavior of the O-rings at different temperatures. They found that at 20 degrees F, the O-rings took over three times as long to seal as at 70 degrees F. This fit with the data they had from inspecting used O-rings; those most likely to be undamaged came from launches in warmer weather.

Four things combined to destroy the *Challenger*.

1. As we have mentioned, the O-rings were not capable of sealing correctly at the low temperatures of January 28.

2. There was a great deal of ice around the *Challenger* that morning due to recent rains and to the fact that certain water systems, such as fire hoses, had been turned on and allowed to run to prevent their freezing. It is possible that water got into the joint and damaged the O-rings when it froze.

3. The heat-resistant putty apparently failed to protect the O-rings from the hot propulsion gases.

4. The SRB sections being used on this flight had been used before, and their dimensions had changed slightly. This slight variation may have prevented the pressure from the combustion gases from helping the O-rings seal correctly.

The government's investigation into the matter came to this conclusion:

> In view of the findings, the Commission concluded that the cause of the Challenger accident was the failure of the pressure seal in the aft field joint of the right Solid Rocket Booster. The failure was due to a faulty design unacceptably sensitive to a number of factors. These factors were the effects of temperature, physical dimensions, the character of materials, the effects of reusability, processing and the reaction of the joint to dynamic loading.[11]

At this point we can start our investigation of the mistakes that made the accident possible. If Thiokol and NASA knew there were problems with the field joints, problems that got worse at low temperatures, why did the launch take place? Didn't anyone pay attention?

Actually they did. When it became known that the launch would take place at record low temperatures, NASA began checking with its contractors to see what problems this would create. Alan McDonald, who directed the SRM project for Thiokol, believed that the cold-weather launch would indeed create problems and directed two of his engineers, Robert Ebeling and Roger Boisjoly, to prepare a presentation on the subject for NASA. The night before the launch a teleconference took place between Morton-Thiokol, management at the Kennedy Space Center, and the Marshall Space Flight Center in Alabama during which the engineers presented their concerns. Unfortunately, they had not had a great deal of time to prepare their material and the data were not conclusive. The engineers showed data on temperature for launches in which O-ring degradation had been found, which seemed to show that the degradation could occur at any temperature, but they did not present data on launches in which no problems occurred, which would have showed a clear relationship with temperature. That is, some flights at low temperatures had O-ring problems and some did not, which made it look like temperature was not a factor; however, no flights at high temperatures had problems, which would have made the situation clear if they had shown that data. Thiokol vice president Bob Lund argued that since there were questions about the joints, it would be imprudent to launch in temperatures so far below what had been done before, but the NASA contingent was more focused on the inconclusive data and believed that the specification for the SRB required it to operate down to 31 degrees F. Actually, the SRB had been tested down to only 40 degrees F because Thiokol believed the 31-degree requirement applied only to time the SRB spent in storage.

NASA clearly wanted to launch. This was an important effort, it had already been delayed several times, and the next launch would be a high-profile mission to investigate Halley's Comet a few days ahead of a rival Soviet probe. NASA wanted to move on to the process of getting ready for that mission. Also, NASA was under severe pressure to get a record number of shuttle flights accomplished that year and show that it could operate efficiently in response to cost competition from the European Space Agency.

Thiokol's group was clearly uncomfortable with the idea of launching in these conditions, and after a lengthy debate one of its senior managers asked to discuss the issue off the teleconference, with only Thiokol personnel. During this discussion, this executive at one point told Lund: "Take off your engineering hat and put on your management hat."[12]

Eventually the managers decided to approve the launch and wrote up a recommendation to that effect, which the engineers refused to sign. Alan McDonald in Florida was surprised at this and also asked NASA management not to launch, but he was overruled.

Temperatures the next day were frigid, and at several points key managers unaware of the O-ring issue had to waive low-temperature limits to continue with the countdown. It is doubtful whether this would have occurred if they had been aware of the controversy surrounding the O-rings.

The government commission that investigated this accident had four findings related to this process, but the important factors are captured in the third and fourth:

> 3. The Commission is troubled by what appears to be a propensity of management at Marshall to contain potentially serious problems and to attempt to resolve them internally rather than communicate them forward. This tendency is altogether at odds with the need for Marshall to function as part of a system working toward successful flight missions, interfacing and communicating with the other parts of the system that work to the same end.

> 4. The Commission concluded that the Thiokol Management reversed its position and recommended the launch of 51-L, at the urging of Marshall and contrary to the views of its engineers in order to accommodate a major customer.[13]

And there you have it. The people with authority at NASA and then at Thiokol had their priorities and did not want to listen to the people who had the expertise. The distance between those with power and those with knowledge was too great. In addition, NASA managers did not communicate the issues up the chain because they did not want to be seen to be the cause of the problem; it would seem too much like admitting a shortcoming. This is the managing-up part of royal thinking.

The pressure on NASA's managers was almost irresistible. They had to deliver the launch, and their job was to eliminate obstacles to it, not create them. In this case they got people to agree to the launch, but that did not change the underlying reality of the hardware.

The pressure on Thiokol was also easy to understand. If they had stuck by a conservative recommendation, it is entirely possible that the NASA managers involved would never have forgiven them.

This case illustrates how instilling an organization with a great drive to reach an important goal can backfire, when that goal becomes so prominent in the work of the people involved that everything else is sacrificed for it. This is a brand of royal thinking in which the royal proclamation is taken too literally by the peasants. You can also see bits of this in the Leeson case. Management set up a situation where making money was the only goal, and paid the price when employees gave them what they asked for at great cost.

Saddam Hussein

There is no more vivid example of the destructive effects of power on rationality than the way Saddam Hussein's brutal treatment of his subordinates led him into catastrophic error during the second Gulf War.

Perhaps this shouldn't be a surprise. If organizational power can have destructive effects on decision making, then we should expect to see some truly irrational behavior in situations where one person has life-and-death power over those around him.

The functioning of Saddam Hussein's political and military team provides a great example of this. In 2006 the U.S. Joint Forces Command (JFCOM) released a report based on interviews with captured Iraqi leaders and official documents that provided insight into the workings of the regime. Most of this case is based on the JFCOM report.[14]

Hussein, of course, was a brutal individual, responsible for millions of deaths through his policies and external wars. His rise to power was punctuated by the murder of his rivals, and his rule was characterized by the almost complete lack of restraint on the whims of the dictator.

However, while hanging people from the ceiling and torturing them may appear to get results, it has its drawbacks as a management technique.

Hussein's character and basic strategy are well known. He was a street-tough thug and assassin, and had risen to power through a combination of skilled politics and ruthless brutality. In his mind, nothing counted but who was standing at the end of the conflict.

The thing that jumps out at a reader of the JFCOM report is how secure Saddam seemed to be in his belief that he would win out eventually. He believed that his commercial allies in France and Russia would use their positions on the United Nations Security Council to prevent an invasion by the United States. Further, supported by a hierarchy of subordinates who were afraid to tell him the truth, he believed that if the United States did invade Iraq, his troops would put up a heroic resistance, bogging American troops down. He was so confident, in fact, that at one point during the war, he told his French and Russian allies (who were attempting to negotiate for the survival of his regime) that he would accept nothing less than "unconditional withdrawal" of American forces because "Iraq is now winning . . . the United States has sunk in the mud of defeat."[15]

Saddam also demonstrated a breathtaking inability to understand his enemies and had little idea of the way Americans thought. According to the JFCOM report:

> From Saddam's point of view the possibility of an American invasion verged on nonsense: After all, America ran away from Vietnam in complete disarray after suffering only slightly more than 58,000 killed in action. Iraq had suffered as many dead in a single battle on the Fao peninsula during the war with Iran.[16]

Saddam viewed America's basic humanity as weakness and was so secure in this view of the world that he was unable to consider that anyone else might have a different one. Certainly the complex interplay of groups and ideas in an atmosphere of relative tolerance that takes place in a modern democracy was foreign to him.

Saddam was his own worst enemy in terms of his decision making. Having determined that he and his apparatus could not be criticized, he punished those who spoke harsh truths and thus prevented his subordinates from bringing him anything but what they thought he wanted to hear. To quote the JFCOM report again:

> Stories circulated widely in the military about generals imprisoned or shot by Saddam personally for transgressions, which included excessive competence or an argumentative nature. Innocence was not a defense: Saddam would announce that he knew when someone was going to betray him, even before that person himself knew it. . . . At one low point in the Iran-Iraq war Saddam asked his ministers for candid advice on what to do. With some temerity the minister of Health suggested that Saddam temporarily step down but resume the presidency after the establishment of peace. Saddam had him carted away immediately. The next day chopped up pieces of the minister's body were delivered to his wife. According to the head of the Military Industrialization Committee, a relative of the murdered minister, "This powerfully concentrated the attention of the other ministers who were unanimous in their insistence that Saddam remain in power."[17]

Even the most senior officials were not immune to punishment if their views did not match the dictator's. Army Chief of Staff Nizar al-Khazraji was fired before the first Gulf War for warning Saddam of the danger of war with the United States. Basically, Saddam did a great job of silencing his subordinates.

This liberal use of punishment created such a focus on accentuating the positive among Saddam's subordinates that no defeat was too crushing to be cast as a victory. The JFCOM report describes a ludicrous scene:

> During one recorded review of the post–Desert Storm study, the Commander of the Republican Guard strode to the podium with confidence and listed the "great" accomplishments of his forces during the "Mother of All Battles," among them:
>
> - Creating impenetrable and perfectly camouflaged command bunkers.
> - Analyzing the battlefield and deploying in such a way as to make the American nuclear-tipped Pershing missiles useless (no mention of the fact that the United States did not deploy Pershing missiles

during the war, or that by dispersing their forces to avoid nuclear attack, the Iraqis became easy prey for the massed Coalition armor).

• Determining the specific method and timing of US operations so that "once the attack began, we were clearly expecting it." (Nothing was in the presentation about how the Iraqis were helped by President Bush giving them an ultimatum and countdown.)[18]

The basic argument here is that "We could have gotten our asses kicked a lot worse, therefore we must have won."

Virtually every aspect of the Iraqi military became colored by the need to feed Saddam only positive news.

At the end of 2000, it came to Saddam's attention that approximately seventy military vehicles were immobile. Saddam told his son Qusay to resolve the problem. Republican Guard mechanics claimed they could repair the vehicles if the funds were made available. Qusay agreed to the work, and funds were provided for the task. Once the work was completed, Qusay sent a representative to inspect the vehicles. The man found them lined up on a vehicle park, thirty-five vehicles on each side. The vehicles looked like new, having been freshly painted and cleaned. After Qusay's representative inspected them, a second inspection was conducted to verify that they were now operational. The staff was told to supply drivers to move all vehicles to the opposite side of the vehicle park to ensure they were in working order. None of the seventy vehicles would start. When Qusay learned this, he instructed that his father not be informed, as he had already told Saddam that the vehicles were operational.[19]

Besides burdening his subordinates with the duty of bringing him only positive news, at the risk of their lives, Saddam meddled extensively in military affairs in which he had little background or talent, thus running afoul of the management distance issue. The JFCOM report describes some of the directions Saddam gave to his soldiers in a training document:

• Train in a way that allows you to defeat your enemy
• Train all units' members in swimming
• Train your soldiers to climb palm trees so that they may use these places for navigation and sniper shooting and
• Train on smart weapons.[20]

Anyone with a military background will recognize the difficulty of getting anything useful out of directions like this. One can imagine the relief of the

Iraqi commanders when they discovered that their aim was to *defeat* the enemy, as opposed to, say, invite him to a nice dinner. And just how were swimming troops to be used?

Similarly, the JFCOM report describes the battle plan trotted out by Saddam's inner circle during the final defense of Baghdad. They divided up the city into concentric rings, the innermost one of which was colored red. The commander of the Second Republican Guard Corps described the plan as follows:

> When Americans arrived at the first ring and on order from Saddam the forces would conduct a simultaneous withdraw. The units would repeat this "procedure" until reaching the red circle. Once in the red circle the remaining units would fight to the death. "I was told that there would be no changes because Saddam had signed the plan already."[21]

The kind of plan a military professional would have created in this situation would have taken into account terrain, supplies, and fields of fire, and provided for detailed procedures for retreating forces. Saddam's approach was childish in its simplicity.

While talented individuals had a hard time under Saddam, others fared better. The JFCOM report describes the career of one of Saddam's cronies.

> One of those at the heart of the regime who proved incapable of providing sound military advice to Qusay was a Major General Barzan 'Abd al-Ghafur, the Commander of the Special Republican Guard. Before the war, Coalition planners generally assumed that the quality—and loyalty—of Iraqi military officers improved as one moved from the militias to the regular Army, to the Republican Guard, and then on to the Special Republican Guard. It stood to reason that the Commander of the Special Republican Guard would then be a highly competent, loyal, and important personality in Iraq's military system. After all, the regime was entrusting that individual with the duty of conducting the final defense of the homes and offices of the regime's elite. Coalition planners considered the Special Republican Guard the elite of the elite; and by logical extension, their commander would surely be the best Saddam could find. This piece of conventional wisdom was wrong.
>
> After the war, the peers and colleagues of the SRG Commander were all openly derisive of Barzan's performance as an officer and commander. Saddam had selected Barzan, as one general noted, because he had several

qualities that Saddam held dear. "He was Saddam's cousin, but he had other important qualities which made him the best man for the job. First, he was not intelligent enough to represent a threat to the regime and second, he was not brave enough to participate in anyone else's plots."

As the SRG commander, Barzan was well aware of the tenuous nature of his position. He recalled in a postwar interview:

> I was called to Baghdad from holiday and told that I would be taking command of the SRG. I was on a probationary status for the first six months. I was ordered by Saddam to take the command; I had no choice. I was sick at the idea of being the SRG commander. It was the most dangerous job in the regime.

When asked in a post-war interview to explain the disparity between the authority he exercised and that exercised by other divisional commanders, the commander answered in an incredulous tone, "I am a Tikriti and other commanders were not." In Saddam's military, tribal or familial relationships trumped the actual documented authority necessary for effective command at any particular echelon.[22]

We can see in this case a number of the pathologies associated with the power and hierarchy in an organization. Saddam's subordinates ceased to inform him of reality; he lost talented individuals and promoted cronyism to an art form. He also meddled in things he didn't understand, to the detriment of his own cause. While the level of power Saddam held over his subordinates was certainly greater than what most managers have over their subordinates, I have seen the same pathologies emerge in relatively normal American business settings more than once.

Montgomery Ward

Some leaders seem to be able to change with the times, while others are apparently convinced that there is only one way to run a business, in any place, time, or industry, and when that script fails they are unable to seek advice or change their minds.

Montgomery Ward and Sears, Roebuck dominated the mail order business in America for most of its existence. Before the advent of the automobile, mail order was a big and glamorous business, as rural Americans ordered their merchandise out of catalogs rather than make difficult trips to urban areas to see the merchandise firsthand. By the mid-1920s Sears was considerably larger than its rival, but Ward was growing more quickly and generally operated at higher margins.

At this time Ward's CEO was Theodore Merseles, an old-school mail order man intent on surpassing Sears. He was convinced he could outstrip Sears in a decade. Merseles's number-two man at this time was Robert Wood. Wood had a much more varied background than Merseles. He had been a quartermaster in the army and director of the Panama Railroad Co. during construction of the Panama Canal. Wood was a visionary. While he had no qualms about making a buck in the mail order business, he also realized that Henry Ford's Model T would enable America's farmers to come into the cities to shop and be less likely to order by mail. He correctly recognized that the future lay in chain department stores, not mail order.

When Sears recruited Wood for its top spot, he jumped at the chance (actually Merseles fired him for talking to Julius Rosenwald at Sears, but then he jumped) and became a retailing legend. He opened a number of stores at Sears and founded Allstate to take advantage of the growing number of cars on the road by insuring them against accidents.

Merseles was a smart guy. He had been trapped a bit by his mail order mind-set, but when he saw the success Sears, Roebuck was having with department stores, he jumped in. There was a brief stumble when Merseles opened his first store. It was actually a showroom; you would look at the merchandise there and then buy from the catalog. However, once he got the hang of it, he started opening stores with a vengeance, peaking at 554 in 1930.

Then the Depression hit, and by 1931 most of his stores were losing money, but he continued to open more. Once Merseles learned a lesson, he didn't forget it. Also, he was known to be an optimistic man, ill suited to the needs of the Depression, which required a more cautious outlook.

With the company's losses mounting, Merseles was replaced with Sewell Avery, the former head of US Gypsum. Avery was admirably suited to run a company during tough times. At US Gypsum he had cut costs and taken the firm into new businesses that had helped it thrive during the cyclical downturns experienced by any industry heavily dependent on construction.

Avery and Ward performed spectacularly. He closed stores that were not performing and opened others; he brought in new managers to dilute the mail order bias that remained part of the company's culture. He introduced pay for performance. In 1931 Ward lost $8.7 million, but by 1933 this had changed into a $2 million profit. By 1939 it had clawed its way back to within reach of Sears, with 80 percent of its rival's revenue.

After World War II, however, Avery's own mythical thinking started to show itself, and his royal thinking kept him from any possibility of breaking out of the box. As a man who had made his name in hard times by cutting costs and hoarding cash, he had a hard time recognizing the postwar boom. In fact, Avery was convinced that there would be a postwar crash. In a 1945 address to shareholders he predicted massive unemployment and depression. Avery tracked economic performance back to the 1800s and insisted that history, not he, was sending the message. He ceased opening stores in 1941.

One might laud Avery for this kind of business scholarship; unfortunately, by 1954 it was obvious to everyone else in the world that the postwar economy was in boom, not bust. At that point Sears had spent $300 million to open 100 new stores since 1946, and Ward had closed 100 in the same period. All its operations were starved for cash, yet the company had huge reserves it was unwilling to spend, hoarding it instead for the anticipated crash. Avery refused to open new stores in areas where the population was growing and didn't even maintain those he had by installing escalators and air conditioning, or even painting them. By 1954 Ward's sales were less than a third those of Sears.

Avery was known as a man devoted to his own opinions; this is where his royal thinking appears. In 1944 he refused to accept a union contract forced on him by the War Labor Board and was carried from his office by soldiers, one of a blessedly small number of incidents of the military being employed against a peaceful citizenry in the history of the United States. In fact, Avery was fairly dismissive of everyone, even his customers. In expanding Ward's merchandise into higher-priced lines, a smart move by itself, he commented that "we no longer depend on hicks and yokels. We sell more than overalls and manure proof shoes."[23]

The company lost immense amounts of executive talent with Avery's high-handed approach. Four presidents and thirty vice presidents resigned due to the pressures of working with a man who simply did not listen to others. Avery once said: "If anyone ventures to differ with me, I throw them out the window."[24]

Which he basically did, frequently purging his executive ranks to avoid any challenge of his decisions. Avery was an archetypical control freak.

When he asked an employee somewhere down the chain of command for a report, he would tell the person not to inform their direct superiors: "You make it direct to me and don't take up the matter with any other official who may be involved."[25]

For a man in his unchallenged position, Avery seemed curiously intent on showing everyone who was boss. He was known to walk around the office loudly telling the world that "I'll show them who runs Wards."[26]

Avery, with his obstinate refusal to take advice, mismanaged Ward for years until the inevitable finally came to pass. In 1955 Avery, now frail and eighty-one years old, fought off a takeover attempt by Lou Wolfson, one of the first "corporate raiders." In this case the best thing for the shareholders would have been for the raider to win, but Avery retained support on Ward's board. It was his last victory.

Avery retired later that year, but the damage had been done. Ward's managerial ranks had been pruned of talent, especially the kind of independent thinkers needed for a rebound. It had fallen hopelessly behind Sears in terms of growth and ended up spending much of Avery's accumulated cash in a vain attempt to catch up. By 1958 Ward still had less than a third of the revenue of Sears and had been passed by J.C. Penney for second place. It seemed to have no focus, buying a concrete water pipe business and a bank.

Unable to recover from the disastrous postwar period and admittedly uninspired management thereafter, Ward eventually filed for bankruptcy in 1997, having lost $249 million in its most recent year of operation.

This case is a mixture of mythical and royal thinking. Certainly Avery was in the grip of his myth of a postwar depression, but his inability to listen to or work with others was broader than that one fixation. Ward's leader was so overconfident in his own opinion that he was simply unable to take advice in any area. He lost immense amounts of executive talent due to his arrogance and generally ran his business into the ground.

Project Alpha

Several of the cases in this chapter are about overconfidence. This case is about being overconfident because you don't realize that you have left your field of expertise and entered another one. This misplaced confidence is illustrated perfectly by the case of Project Alpha.

Project Alpha was about scientifically evaluating claims of psychic power and paranormal phenomena. It may be surprising to some that this kind of activity is still going on, but it is, and some of it is being done by reasonably well credentialed scientists.

From the beginning, the people who have done this kind of testing have largely been physical scientists, physicists, and psychologists. The reasoning goes that these people know how to design experiments and to ferret out the truth when dealing with the natural world and therefore should be able to do so with a human subject. Unfortunately, this is a classic case of bringing a knife to a gunfight; in practice, the physicists have made a fairly poor showing. It's not that they don't know how to test; it's that they don't know how to test someone who might try to cheat. Time after time respected scientists have come forward with ringing declarations about the legitimacy of a particular psychic, only to see that person caught cheating soon after and discredited. The best investigations of this kind involve professional conjurers, or stage magicians, as well as scientists, and the dangers of undertaking such an investigation without this kind of counsel have been well known for decades. But some scientists apparently can't imagine that they can be fooled by anything as simple as stage magic and still resist the fairly clear evidence of history.

In 1979 James McDonnell, chairman of McDonnell-Douglas Aircraft, announced that he had awarded a $500,000 grant to Washington University of St. Louis to establish the McDonnell Laboratory for Psychical Research. This laboratory was the beginning—or perhaps it would be better to call it the target—of Project Alpha.

Project Alpha was the brainchild of James Randi, a stage magician heavily involved in the debunking of fake psychics, who believed that the scientific world needed a lesson in how to test psychic claimants. The result was a wonderful example of the limitations of degreed and respected academics when forced to think outside their field of expertise.

Randi, by the way, is not your everyday professional puller of rabbits from hats. He is a past winner of a MacArthur Fellowship, or "genius award," for his investigations of psychic phenomena. He has written eleven books on related subjects and still offers a $1 million reward to anyone who can demonstrate a paranormal power in a controlled test. I have seen Randi perform on several occasions and can testify that he is a lot of fun to watch.

Randi recruited two young magicians who had shown interest in his work as a skeptical investigator of the paranormal, and when the McDonnell Laboratory advertised for subjects for its psychic testing, these two young men responded to the ads. They were Steve Shaw, an eighteen-year-old hospital employee from Washington, and Michael Edwards, a student from Marion, Iowa. Both men were accepted, out of over 300 applicants, for investigation by the McDonnell lab.

Randi provided Dr. Peter Phillips, the director of the lab and a physicist, with a detailed list of eleven items to beware of in testing psychic claimants and suggested that a stage magician be present for the activity. He even offered himself in this role at his own expense, but Phillips did not accept his offer. The lab did use some equipment designed by an amateur magician, who assured them that it was tamperproof, but this was no substitute for having a professional in attendance.

Randi, Shaw, and Edwards agreed ahead of time that if the young men were ever asked by an experimenter if they were using trickery, they would immediately admit it and say that Randi had sent them, but they were never asked.

When Shaw and Edwards got to the laboratory, they immediately took control. If the conditions for a test were not to their liking, they would throw a tantrum and get them changed. This is an important part of fooling a psychic investigator; stage magic thrives on chaos, or at least lack of control. Stage magic relies on psychology and sleight-of-hand to create its illusions, and carefully controlled environments make this difficult. An uncontrolled environment is exactly what the conjuror ordered.

For most physicists who have never studied the subject, trying to figure out what a good stage magician is doing as he's doing it is kind of like a college professor challenging a professional boxer in the ring. You are playing the other guy's game; you will certainly lose, and most probably you will be made to look ridiculous.

Phillips and his band of researchers actually made it worse than that. Not only did they let the claimants take over the lab, but they ignored Randi's cautions. For instance, Randi had warned them not to allow the subjects access to multiple test objects (such as spoons or keys to be bent using psychic power) at any time. The lab laid out a number of objects, most of which were marked with paper tags on bits of string. The young magicians had no trouble switching tags between the precisely measured objects so that when a given object was remeasured, it would appear to have been bent even though it was actually an entirely different item.

In a good example of the kind of thing a professional conjuror would have prevented, Shaw beat the Ph.D.'s in a test where the object was to bend a small metal rod. Here is Randi's account:

> One rather naive experiment, conducted with Steve Shaw, involved a small slab of clear acrylic plastic in which a shallow groove had been cut. Into this groove was placed a thin (about 1/16) metal rod a few inches long that fit loosely, flush with the surface. It was believed, and so stated, that it was not possible to remove the rod from the groove by hand without either overturning the slab or using a tool of some sort. Steve was asked to stroke the metal with his finger and cause it to bend. He quickly discovered that the rod tilted up and out of the groove when he pressed down upon one end, the flesh of his finger having squeezed into the groove. He simply removed the rod unnoticed, bent it slightly, and re-inserted it into the groove, lying it on its side, since the groove was wide enough to accommodate the bend. Then he stroked and rotated the rod 90 degrees to make it appear to bend up and out of the groove. The feat was deemed impossible by trickery.[27]

The central problem here is the misplaced confidence by the intelligent Ph.D.'s running the test.

After the investigation had been going on for some time, and the investigators were completely convinced of the legitimacy of their two stars' psychic ability, Randi leaked some hints about the operation at a magician's conference. Soon afterward he received a call from Phillips asking for help. Randi provided Phillips with a videotape showing how a number of typical psychic tricks are done, and Phillips showed that tape along with one of Edwards and Shaw at a convention. After the convention, according to Randi:

> Phillips was cornered by me after the workshop, and I insisted upon showing him and Mark Shafer, his principal researcher, where the tape showed evidence of fraud. Visibly shaken, the two thanked me for my efforts, and I parted from them reasonably sure that they had been impressed enough to change their ways.[28]

Indeed they had been. Edwards and Shaw reported that the experimental control tightened up considerably after that and the amount of psychic activity dropped off in proportion. This proves that if you are reasonably honest with yourself, you can work your way back from being deeply in error, but only if you are willing to believe the evidence when it presents itself, as Phillips was, to his credit. Other psychic researchers were not as able in this regard, or perhaps they just hadn't had the benefit of Randi's one-on-one coaching. Shaw and Edwards became much-sought-after subjects for other researchers up until the day they made the hoax public. Even after the truth came out, there were still a few true believers who asked, "How do these kids know they don't have psychic powers?" Thus showing an interesting element of mythical thinking in this case.

The element that I want to emphasize here is the misplaced confidence of the smart researchers who thought that because they were good at one thing, they would be good at something else completely unrelated to it. It is interesting that in the area of physical skills, this confusion does not occur. Nobody expects great football players to be great baseball players, or great boxers to be great wrestlers. This may be because we have never seen anyone perform at the highest levels in two or more completely unrelated physical activities (Bo Jackson aside). In the mental realm, we see only that a person is intelligent and fail to recognize that his skill in one area might not translate into skill in another, and that it is no sin to turn to an expert when asked to play a game you don't understand.

In Closing

Some psychologists have been predicting for years now that the age of cognitive science is finally upon us. They have said that we are now ready to recognize that the most important and difficult aspect of existence that we can attempt to engineer is our own thinking. In this view of the world, humanity is about to enter a new age. The information age will give way to the age of cognition, and we will build decision processes with the same precision that in the past we have used in building bridges, airplanes, and computers.

I can't say if these people are correct; I suspect that they are overstating the case. Like everyone else, they are capable of wishful thinking. But I do think that we have reached the point where almost any mass of data, if it exists and if it's important enough, can be made available to a decision maker. How we analyze that data, and how we derive from it information and wisdom will depend on how well we think about how we think.

I also find it hopeful that for every failure documented here and elsewhere there is a corresponding stroke of genius, and for every trap we fall into, there seems to be at least one we avoid. Human beings are nothing if not persistent, and I have no doubt that, as bumpy as the road will be, eventually we'll figure out how we want to think.

■ NOTES

1. S. Milgrom, "Behavioral Study of Obedience," *Journal of Abnormal and Social Psychology* 67 (1963).
2. Judith Rawnsley, *Total Risk: Nick Leeson and the Fall of Barings Bank* (New York: HarperCollins, 1995).
3. Nick Leeson, *Rogue Trader: How I Brought Down Barings Bank and Shook the Financial World* (London: Little Brown, 1996).
4. Judith Rawnsley, *Total Risk: Nick Leeson and the Fall of Barings Bank* (New York: HarperCollins, 1995).
5. Ibid.
6. Ibid.
7. Ibid.
8. Ibid.
9. Ibid.
10. Judith Rawnsley, *Total Risk: Nick Leeson and the Fall of Barings Bank* (New York: HarperCollins, 1995).
11. The Presidential Commission on the Space Shuttle *Challenger* Accident Report, June 6, 1986.
12. Ibid.
13. Ibid.
14. Kevin Woods, Michael R. Pease, Mark E. Stout, Williamson Murray, and James G. Lacey. *Iraqi Perspectives Project: A View of Operation Iraqi Freedom from Saddam's Senior Leadership* (2006).
15. Ibid.
16. Ibid.
17. Ibid.
18. Ibid.
19. Ibid.
20. Ibid.
21. Ibid.
22. Ibid.
23. Robert Soble, *When Giants Stumble* (Englewood Cliffs, NJ: Prentice Hall, 1999).
24. Ibid.
25. Ibid.
26. Ibid.
27. James Randi, "The Project Alpha Experiment: Part 1. The First Two Years," *Skeptical Inquirer* 7, no. 4 (Summer 1983).
28. Ibid.

References and Further Reading

CHAPTER 1 AVOIDING ERROR: AN INTRODUCTION

CHAPTER 2 WISHFUL THINKING

Mackay, Charles. *Extraordinary Popular Delusions and the Madness of Crowds*. New York: Crown Publishers, 1980.

McCoy, Bob. *Quack!: Tales of Medical Fraud from the Museum of Questionable Medical Devices*. Santa Monica, CA: Santa Monica Press LLC, 2000.

Murray, Williamson. *The Change in the European Balance of Power, 1938–1939*. Princeton, NJ: Princeton University Press, 1984.

Rock, William R. *Neville Chamberlain*. New York: Twayne Publishers, 1969.

CHAPTER 3 MYTHICAL THINKING

Brunner, J. S., and L. J. Postman. "On the Perception of Incongruity: A Paradigm," *Journal of Personality* 18 (1949): 206–223.

Deutsch, M., and H. B. Gerard. "A Study of Normative and Informational Social Influences upon Individual Judgement," *Journal of Abnormal and Social Psychology* 51 (1955): 629–636.

Galling, W., and R. Ball. "How Omega and Tissot Got Ticking Again," *Fortune*, January 14, 1980.

Mosteller, Frederick. "Innovation and Evaluation," *Science* 211: 881–886, 02/1981.

Rogers, Everett. *Diffusion of Innovations*. New York: The Free Press, 1995.

Soble, Robert. *When Giants Stumble*. Englewood Cliffs, NJ: Prentice-Hall, 1999.

Ternov, Sven. "The Human Side of Medical Mistakes." In Patrice Spath (ed.), *Error Reduction in Health Care*. Hoboken, NJ: Jossey-Bass, 2000.

■ CHAPTER 4 TRIBAL THINKING

American Anthropological Association Statement on Race: www.aaanet.org/stmts/racepp.htm.

David, Saul. *Military Blunders: The How and Why of Military Failure*. New York: Carroll & Graf, 1998.

Finan, William, and Annette LaMond. "Sustaining U.S. Competitiveness in Microelectronics: The Challenge to U.S. Policy." In Bruce Scott and George Lodge (eds.), *U.S. Competitiveness in the World Economy*. Boston: Harvard Business School Press.

Harari, Oren. "The Eleventh Reason Why TQM Doesn't Work," *Management Review* 82, No. 1 (January 1993).

Hyuczynski, Andrzej A. *Management Gurus: What Makes Them and How to Become One*. London: International Thomson Publishing, 1996.

Kellaway, Lucy. "Volumes in Learning—Take It as Read," *Financial Times* (London), September 12, 1995.

Kirkpatrick, Lyman. "The Inspector General's Survey of the Cuban Operation," February 21, 1998. www.foia.cia.gov/ 2-16-62.

Kerr, N. L., and R. J. MacCoun. "The Effects of Jury Size and Polling Method on the Process and Product of Jury Deliberation," *Journal of Personality and Social Psychology* 48 (1985): 349–363.

rastafarian.net/what_is_melanin.htm.

Staw, Barry M., and Lisa D. Epstein. "What Bandwagons Bring: Effects of Popular Management Techniques on Corporate Performance, Reputation, and CEO Pay," *Administrative Science Quarterly*, No. 3 (September 2000): 523–556.

Suedfeld, P., S. Bochner, and C. Matas. "Petitioner's Attire and Petition Signing by Peace Demonstrators: A Field Experiment," *Journal of Applied Social Psychology* 1 (1971): 278–283.

Tajfel, H. *Human Groups and Social Categories*. Cambridge, UK: Cambridge University Press. 1981.

Warren, Ward W. "Inspector General: Master of All He Surveys," *Periscope* 22, No. 2 (1998): 6–7.

■ CHAPTER 5 ROYAL THINKING

Lane, Brian. *Killer Cults: Murderous Messiahs and Their Fanatical Followers*. London: Headline Book Publishing, 1996.

Russo, J. Edward, and J. H. Paul Shoemaker. *Decision Traps: The Ten Barriers to Brilliant Decision-Making and How to Overcome Them*. New York: Fireside, 1990.

Stone, Dan N. "Overconfidence in Initial Self Efficacy Judgments: Effects on Decision Processes and Performance," *Organizational Behavior and Human Decision Processes* 59 (1994): 452–474.

Index